DON'T YOU
BELIEVE IT!

by John Radford

illustrated by Donald Rooum

DON'T YOU BELIEVE IT!

*some things everybody knows
that actually AIN'T SO*

Drawn from the Best Sources for the
AMUSEMENT AND INSTRUCTION
of the general Public by

John Radford

And illustrated by
Donald Rooum

2007

Published in 2007 by
Stepney Green Press
email j.k.radford@btinternet.com

© 2007
John Radford and Donald Rooum

ISBN 978-0-9554431-0-7

Designed by Donald Rooum and Jayne Clementson
Typeset by Jayne Clementson

Printed in Great Britain by Biddles Ltd,
24 Rollesby Road, Hardwick Industrial Estate, Kings Lynn, Norfolk PE30 4LS

INDEX OF TOPICS

PREFACE

All right, all right, I know! They aren't things that *everybody* knows, if you want to be difficult. You and I, Dear Reader, both know better, do we not? But as Bernard Shaw is alleged to have said, when a member of the audience booed one of his first nights, 'I agree with you, my dear sir. But who are we two against so many?'

What follows are all topics that I think are often misunderstood, to say the least. And as an academic I have an occupational urge to put them right. There is no particular link between them, though they do to some extent reflect my own interests. On the whole I have followed the old Army rule and avoided sex, religion and politics, even though the last two consist largely of things that 'ain't so', in my opinion. And Donald agrees.

Why fifty-six topics? It seemed enough. Mr Heinz did very well out of fifty-seven. In fact, by the time he thought of the slogan he already had more than fifty-seven varieties. Actually there are more than fifty-six as some include related items. 'Ostriches' includes elephants, lemmings and swans. 'Kilts' includes bowler hats. And so on. Obvious, really.

I have done my very best to get the facts right but I apologise in advance for anything that turns out to be wrong. I have not included a scholarly list of references but I have mentioned some key books or web sites where I thought they might be of interest.

The Index of Topics is just that. It does not tell what all the erroneous beliefs are, but it does enable one to find an item, for example when you in turn want to bore someone with it. As I see it, the book is for browsing, for filling in odd moments when you might better be brushing up your Greek, or like Bertie Wooster completing the crossword with a shrewd 'emu' in the top right hand corner ('large Australian bird, three letters'). Or planning how to spend the lottery millions which will surely arrive any day now, etc.

So, if you will, browse. If you don't like the text, Donald Rooum's pictures alone are worth the money. And I hope you enjoy it as much as I have.

John Radford
London, 2006

9

1

KING ALFRED BURNT THE CAKES
Or did he? Anyway, what and whose were the cakes, and what did it matter?

This is one of those that, it seems, will run and run. Generations of school children have heard the story, and been told to draw various lessons from it. A glance at the internet shows it is still going strong, in many versions, including one in Norwegian and another in Chinese, without the slightest suggestion that it is anything other than historical fact. They are embellished with circumstantial details and extra dialogue, and made to carry various moral messages, usually concerned with humility and duty.

Who was Alfred?
Alfred the Great lived from 849 to 899, becoming king of Wessex in 871. His kingdom was, ultimately, roughly the south and west of England. Reliable historical records from this period are few. It is well established, however, that Alfred was able to stem the

attacks of successive Danish invaders and secure his kingdom. A line from Chester to London marks the limits of the 'Danelaw'.

Alfred did this by fighting, by building fortifications and creating a naval force, and also by diplomacy. He was clearly an impressive leader who lived long in folk memory. He is the only British monarch to receive the popular and lasting appellation of 'the Great' (although it does not seem to appear in writing before the seventeenth century). Alfred also instituted a code of laws and fostered education – a rarity at the time.

Origins of the story

The origins of the story of the cakes are complex. They are explored in exhaustive – though not exhausting, it is a real whodunnit – detail by Alfred P. Smyth in his magisterial *King Alfred the Great* (1995) and later in *The Mediaeval Life of King Alfred the Great* (2002). What seems clear is that the first written version occurs in a *Life* of St Neot, an otherwise rather obscure saint whose name survives as that of a town in Huntingdonshire, where there was a monastery called after him. It was written probably some time between 1000 and 1050, a century after Alfred.

In this book, Alfred is somewhat of a supporting character. The cakes story is that, in 878, in retreat from the Danes, Alfred is holed up on the isle of Athelney in the marshes of Somerset. Venturing out in disguise, he finds himself in the home of a swineherd, whose wife is making bread. She leaves the loaves (cakes is just an alternative word) on the hearth, and Alfred fails to notice they are burning. When the woman returns, she upbraids him, saying that he is too careless to attend to the bread, but quick enough to eat it once it's baked.

An alternative version appears in a work known as the *Annals of St Neots*, written about 1020-35. In this, the swineherd is a cowherd, and more importantly, Alfred is distracted by working on his bow and arrows and other weapons. In modern versions this often changes into worrying about his war plans. After this it gets a bit complicated. The most famous early life of Alfred was attributed to one Asser, who was Bishop of Sherborne in Dorset, and a contemporary. At the Dissolution of the monasteries which

Henry VIII instigated, a great many manuscripts, as well as other treasures, were destroyed. Copies were in any case few. As it happened, Matthew Parker, who was Archbishop of Canterbury from 1559 to 1575, was interested in historical records and preserved a good many of them. A few he caused to be printed, and one of these was Asser's life of Alfred, in 1574.

Complications

Parker seems to have chosen this because Asser could be seen as an ancient British bishop, and Alfred as an Anglo-Saxon and a devout king, and thus a fore-runner of the Protestant and nationalist King Henry. Parker also had the *Annals of St Neots*, and he believed this was also by Asser. In this he followed the man who discovered the *Annals* when the monastery was dissolved in 1539, the antiquary John Leland. Parker, however, did not just print what he had. His aim was to make the best version he could. He had experts on his staff who could imitate old manuscripts, and he and they certainly altered some. In particular he apparently inserted the cakes story into Asser's life. It is now hard to be certain, because the only surviving mediaeval copy of that life was lost in a fire in 1731.

Even this may not be the end of it. Smyth argues plausibly, though controversially, that the Asser life was not by Asser at all, but was written a century later by a monk, Byrhtferth of Ramsey, who may also have written the *Life of St Neot*. In any case, the cakes story, as it appears in the latter, was simply a folk-tale, or else made up by the author. Smyth points out that this version involves a common folk theme, that of role reversal. The reason that Alfred neglects the bread is not that he is preoccupied; it is that he is a king, and such a menial task is impossible for him. But when rallied on it, in order to preserve his disguise, he has to adopt a subservient role and accept his scolding. It is nothing to do with humility. In the *Annals* version, on the other hand, he gives the game away by working on his weapons.

Well, you pays your money and you takes your choice. It still remains possible that the story originated in a real incident. But it survived, no doubt, because it fitted in with the folk memory of a good and wise king, not too proud to accept a housewife's rebuke.

2

'ANARCHY' AND 'ANARCHISM' MEAN DISORGANIZED CHAOS AND POINTLESS DISRUPTION

and anarchists are either lawless yobs, or more sinisterly people intent on assassination or blowing things up

Not infrequently, the mass media report that 'anarchists' are intending to disrupt some international meeting of governments or business, or have partially managed to do so. There are pictures of more or less wild looking individuals breaking down barriers, or struggling (usually unsuccessfully) with police. The common view seems to be correct. In Roget's *Thesaurus* we find grouped together 'revolutionary, anarchist, nihilist, terrorist, revolutionist'.

Against authority
From a linguistic point of view, the problem is that there is no legal, or even generally accepted, definition of 'anarchist'. Many people of varying opinions and attitudes call themselves, or are called by others, 'anarchists'. Most would agree, however, that the root of the meaning is the original Greek one, absence or rejection

of authority. Some would qualify this as 'imposed authority'. This however has led into many and various pathways.

No doubt since human beings first became social beings and aware of themselves, some have been leaders, often by force, indeed this is characteristic of some non-human species too. But others have rejected authority, either preferring untrammelled individualism, or seeking co-operative organisation on a basis of equality. Some have seen the origins of anarchism as a philosophy in ancient Chinese Daoism. Others point to such movements as the seventeenth century Diggers and Levellers. But most historians (e.g. Peter Marshall, in *Demanding the Impossible: A History of Anarchism*, 1992), find the beginnings of anarchism as a system in the French Revolution of 1789. But we know, as Lady Bracknell put it, to what that unfortunate movement led; like so many violent upsets, a worse tyranny than it replaced.

The first anarchist?
The first person to formulate a recognisably anarchist programme was William Godwin (1756-1836), famous in his day but now largely forgotten. He argued that happiness for all can only be attained by a society that is rational and just; and this depends on the capacity of human beings for progressive improvement, ultimately for perfectibility – 'one of the most unequivocal characteristics of the human species'. He was an extreme environmentalist: it is society that makes us what we are. We can, then, become slaves, or free men. The latter is the rational choice. Some subsequent thinkers have argued, or assumed, that humans are innately good, so that all that is needed is to let them develop naturally, without the constraints of authority.

The charge of naivety has been levelled against anarchist thinkers (sometimes by those taking the even more absurd view that we are all innately bad, as in the Christian doctrine of 'original sin'). Science today makes it increasingly clear that, in fact, every individual has potential for both good and bad, however these are defined, although in different proportions in each case. And this potential interacts in complex ways with environmental influences. We have enough evidence to be confident of some general principles for better development. We can foster abilities for rational thinking, responsibility, sensitivity to others, co-operation, control of violence and so on, which on balance make for wiser individuals and a more satisfactory society.

Varieties

In practice, those of a broadly anarchist persuasion have produced many variations around the central theme. Indeed the very rejection of authority makes diversity inevitable. It is the opposite of a dictatorship which all must obey, or a dogmatic religion to which all must subscribe. Thus some accept some form of religion, though most perhaps reject it. Some have favoured, or tolerated, the use of violent methods, though again most probably reject these.

Another variation is between those who feel that the way forward is a complete overthrow of the existing authoritarian systems of state and church, and those who seek rather to 'build a new society within the framework of the old', making advances towards autonomy and self-government wherever possible. Yet again, some favour a back-to-nature, ecological approach, others point to the potentially liberating power of scientific knowledge (for example, recently, the explosion of information on the World Wide Web – which governments are not slow to seek to control).

Most of these variations are not, in fact, incompatible with each other. They are all informed by the general principle that it is better that human beings are in charge of their own affairs, and responsible for their own actions, individually and collectively, rather than being subject to the power of other persons or institutions. Most 'anarchists' would probably hold that it is the latter that are, far and away, responsible for violence and aggression; and that the sort of society that they wish to see would be far more productively organised than the one we have now. Imposed control would be replaced, not by chaos, but by self control.

My own belief is that education and psychology, the disciplines of my professional life, exemplify and support an anarchist approach. Both are essentially about increasing informed, responsible choice. But that must wait for another time.

3

KING ARTHUR AND HIS KNIGHTS OF THE ROUND TABLE FOUGHT ON HORSEBACK IN HEAVY ARMOUR

using lance, sword and shield, and lived in great castles complete with turrets, battlements and drawbridges.

The Matter of Britain, as the Arthurian stories have long been known, is of course legend. In fact it is an amalgamation of many legends, with many sources. Some of these were tales of the exploits of chivalrous or dastardly knights, told or retold by romancers and poets. Some were religious or mystical, such as the notion of the Holy Grail, the ultimate goal of knightly quests, both physical and spiritual in nature. Some experts consider this was invented by the author of the first written account of it, Chretien de Troyes, about 1280, others feel it drew on older sources. In its Christian incarnation, it was the cup from which the disciples drank at the Last Supper, and in which, perhaps, some of Christ's blood was

17

collected at the crucifixion, brought to Glastonbury by Joseph of Arimathea. But it may stem also from non- or pre-Christian sources as an ever-full vessel, a cornucopia. The word 'grail' itself originally meant a dish used for successive courses of a meal.

Yet other legends concerned Merlin, the prophet and magician. As we have him, he seems to be largely the creation of Geoffrey of Monmouth, in his *Historia Regum Britanniae* which was written about 1135, and *Vita Merlini* (c. 1150). But he too drew on folk tales, some of them about a wild man of the woods, others about some kind of inspired or magically gifted person (even perhaps what is now very loosely called a 'shaman'). And still another theme centres on Camelot, capital of a realm of peace and prosperity yet threatened by dark forces.

Was there a 'real' Arthur?

Then there is Arthur himself. The earliest written account of him, in the *Historia Brittonum* written in Wales about 829-830, has him as a 'battle-leader' (*dux bellorum*), rather than a king. After that, some stories tell of what might perhaps have been real battles that became legends. Others give him an other-worldly quest like that for the Grail; still others speak of him as immortal. Many attempts have been made to find the 'real' Arthur. It cannot be done, the evidence is simply not there. But it is not unreasonable to speculate that one source may indeed be a real man, or even more than one. Such a figure might be a leader who, after the Roman legions had left Britain, and Rome itself had fallen to the barbarians in 410, fought against the Saxon invaders, and perpetuated some memory of a vanished age of civilisation.

There is even historical evidence that in the course of the fifth century, a period of widespread raiding was followed by a respite and a partial recovery. There is also a small but perhaps significant clue in the name. Arthur is the Welsh form of a Roman name, Artorius. It seems unlikely that a purely imaginary character, long after Roman times, should have acquired a Roman name.

Malory's Arthur

All these themes and more circulated in many varieties through the Middle Ages, taking on such forms as the customs of the day, or the imagination of story-tellers, might suggest. Arthur and his knights as we have them result mainly from one version, that of Sir Thomas Malory, who probably lived from about 1416 to 1471 (it is not absolutely certain which of several Thomas Malorys he was). He called his long book *Le Morte d'Arthur*, the death of Arthur, and seems to have composed it while in prison, finishing it about 1469. A damaged manuscript copy was discovered in Winchester College in 1934, and there is a complete printed one, by William Caxton, dating from 1485. Both are versions of an earlier original.

Malory's book is the origin of Tennyson's Arthurian poems and of most of the subsequent re-tellings, including perhaps the most powerful, *The Once and Future King*, (1938-58) by T.H. White, on which the musical Camelot was loosely based. Malory, like others before him, gave Arthur and the knights a more or less contemporary setting, very far from what had been the case when the stories began to be widespread, or when some original of Arthur possibly lived. Heavy armour, jousts and tournaments, elaborate heraldry and ritual, fortified castles, had reached about their maximum development, soon to be overtaken by artillery, new forms of warfare and social organisation, indeed a New World (only twenty years after Malory, Columbus reached America), though many features lingered on in some form as indeed they still do.

Arthur today

The mass media, in particular films and later television, have enthusiastically adopted, and freely adapted, a romanticised mediaevalism for Arthur and many other new adventures of a vaguely Arthurian nature. With Hollywood's cheerful disregard for any notion of historical accuracy, such epics are not of Malory's, nor Arthur's, nor anyone else's time, but are pure fantasies. And indeed one may ask, why not? Legends are under no obligation to correspond to material reality. If they survive, it is not as history, though they may be confused with it, but as stories that embody human desires and emotions – adventures, magic, victory and defeat, love and despair and all the rest.

4

THE BATTLE OF WATERLOO WAS WON ON THE PLAYING FIELDS OF ETON

according to the Duke of Wellington.

Sometimes the Iron Duke is supposed to have said this immediately on winning, sometimes years later; sometimes he is alleged to have written it. There is actually no evidence for any of these. And it seems an unlikely opinion. Wellington did attend Eton, but only for a short time (1781-1784), and didn't think much of it. He was a lonely boy, and had no gift for Greek and Latin, which were the staple of the curriculum. He played mostly alone, often amusing himself by practicing jumping, particularly over a convenient ditch.

Eton College

But was Waterloo so won? Hardly. Obviously the vast mass of troops were not schooled at Eton, indeed very little anywhere. Some of the officers certainly were, but not in the way the phrase suggests and which seems to have become a myth. In 2002 for example, Charles Barnes in the *Florida State Times* quoted the famous phrase and added: 'Boys who were destined to become leaders of the officer corps were drilled in discipline, hardiness, teamwork and other virtues in closely supervised games of sport in England's elite military academy'.

Eton College was founded in 1440 by Henry VI, mainly to educate, free, seventy 'King's Scholars'. But like other 'public' schools, it developed into a fee-paying private, or as they are now called 'independent' school. By Wellington's time it had long been elite, but it has never been a military academy.

And in Wellington's day there was almost nothing in the way of organised sport, and no formal playing fields. Boys played games as they always have, but mostly these were rough and ready affairs. The only team game in England with anything approaching agreed rules was cricket. A set of Laws was formulated in 1727 (other games have rules, cricket has Laws), but even then regional variations continued. Eton only began to play its great rival Harrow in 1805, twenty years after Wellington left.

Victorian games

The games ethos of public schools is a late Victorian invention. Dr Arnold, the famous Headmaster of Rugby from 1827 to 1842, had no time for sport, and when Dr Moberley of Winchester spoke of 'idle' boys, he meant those playing cricket. Sport began to take hold in the mid-nineteenth century, and by the end of it was an almost religious cult. It came to stand for, and was believed to inculcate, the qualities of leadership, duty and fair play. The essence is expressed in Sir Henry Newbolt's 1897 poem 'Vitai Lampada': *There's a breathless hush in the Close tonight...* while later in the second verse *...the voice of a schoolboy rallies the ranks / 'Play up! Play up, and play the game!'*

Wellington revisited the school thirty-four years after leaving it, and he did then remark that he thought his 'spirit of enterprise' owed something to his solitary sport. Three years after his death in 1852, a French writer, Count de Montalembert, visiting Eton, apparently heard of this remark, and turned it into the Duke saying: *'C'est ici qu'a gagné la bataille de Waterloo'* (It is here that the battle of Waterloo was won). Somewhere along the line Wellington's school experiences came to be re-interpreted by the values of a century later. As so often happens, the present was given a false aura of a venerable history, and the prestige of the country's most famous general.

5

BLONDIN CROSSED NIAGARA FALLS ON A TIGHTROPE

Who was he? When did he do it? Have others done it?

To be honest right away, this is almost true. No one has, to date, actually crossed the Falls on a rope or wire. The crossings have been done over the Niagara Gorge, that is downstream of the Falls. Blondin wanted to do it higher up, but the owner of the land refused, for fear of an accident. But the Falls appear in many reference sources. Maybe the name Blondin is not so widely known now. But the achievement is worth re-telling.

Blondin at the Falls
Niagara Falls had begun to be a tourist attraction after the end of the 1812 war between America and Britain. By the 1820s there were three hotels for visitors. Blondin, sometimes called Charles or Chevalier Blondin, crossed first on 30th June 1859, and subsequently sixteen times more on different occasions. And in different ways, including carrying his manager, Harry Colcord, piggyback, as he did subsequently in other places.

He also did it blindfolded, and in a sack, and on stilts, and pushing a wheelbarrow. And one time he carried a stove, on which in the middle he made an omelette, which he ate before continuing. I don't know how big the stove was. One would be inclined to doubt his feats, except that they were witnessed by thousands, at Niagara and elsewhere. Blondin's rope (or wire) was reported to be 7.5 cm in diameter. It was 160 feet above the water, and some 1,100 feet long.

Who was Blondin?

Rope walking has been practiced for many centuries. There are records of such acrobatics two thousand years ago in China. (It doesn't, at first sight, seem one of the most obvious things for human beings to attempt, unless, one wildly speculates, it reflects some ancestral memory of our life in the trees.) But surely Blondin must be the all-time champion. His real name was Jean Francois Gravelet. He was born in 1824 at St Omer in France. At the age of five he saw his first rope walker, and (it is said) immediately attempted it himself between two chairs (don't try this at home!). His father, an acrobat, sent him to the Gymnastic School at Lyon, and six months later he made his professional debut, as 'The Little Wonder'. He took his name from the proprietor of a circus in which he worked. He went on to perform with P.T. Barnum's 'Greatest Show on Earth', before branching out on his own.

His career was, it seems, one of unbroken success. He habitually performed in situations in which a fall would almost certainly have been fatal. At Glasgow in 1861, for example, he walked on a 300 foot long rope, 70 feet above the ground. And as usual he was not content with walking, but turned somersaults and stood on his head, as well as carrying his long-suffering manager on his back (not all at the same time). The crowd was estimated at 10,000 (but crowd estimates are very often inaccurate.) A contemporary poster advertises him as appearing 'On the high rope, wet or dry', with an admission charge of one shilling (five pence in today's currency).

No more crossings?

The Niagara crossing made Blondin world-famous, and his fees were large. In 1861 and 1862 he performed in the Crystal Palace, the vast iron and glass edifice built by Joseph Paxton for the Great Exhibition of 1851. He was paid £1,200 for twelve performances – today, at least £10,000 per performance. At the first of the 1862 shows he had his young daughter, aged five, 180 feet up on the wire with him, in a wheelbarrow, scattering flowers on the crowd below. This caused protests, and the Home Secretary of the day forbade a repetition.

In his heyday Blondin was said to earn half a million dollars a year (of the order of ten million pounds today). Not the least remarkable fact is that he went on performing into old age, and died in his bed. After a break in the 1880s he returned to the wire, and his last appearance was in 1896. The following year he died of diabetes, at his home in Northfields, Ealing, London.

After Blondin, other daredevils walked wires across the Niagara Gorge fairly regularly during the rest of the nineteenth century. But since then there seem to have been only two crossings, in 1911 and 1975. Numerous persons have gone over the Falls, in boats or barrels or on rafts, often with fatal results.

Blondin's feats make him seem like some freak of nature. Maybe it is just that if there is a demand for any sort of achievement, sooner or later some individual will set a standard that is never matched, until changing circumstances make it unlikely to be repeated.

6

IF YOU WANT TO EAT WELL IN ENGLAND, YOU SHOULD TAKE BREAKFAST THREE TIMES A DAY
Conversely, there is the pathetic 'continental breakfast' which consists of coffee and a roll or a croissant.

The first remark is attributed to the writer W. Somerset Maugham (1874-1965) (though I have seen it fathered on Dr Johnson, as so often happens). That there is still some belief in it is suggested by the number of establishments that proudly boast a 'full English breakfast'. But what is this glorious feast? It means, today, simply a fry-up, a plate with some selection of, usually, bacon, sausage, egg, tomato, mushrooms and perhaps a slice of black pudding, more or less ample. Otherwise the meal consists of the usual toast and tea or coffee.

A Beeton breakfast
It is a far cry from the Victorian menu which doubtless inspired the remark. Mrs Isabella Beeton, the young housewife who produced her book of *Household Management* in 1861, and whose name still resonates on the covers of cookery books, many having no connection with her, suggested for breakfast:

...broiled fish such as mackerel, whiting, herrings or dried haddocks, mutton chops, rump steaks, broiled sheep's kidneys, kidneys a la maitre d'hotel, sausages, plain rashers of bacon, bacon and poached eggs, ham and poached eggs, omelets, plain boiled eggs, poached eggs on toast, collared and potted meats or fish, cold game and poultry, veal and ham pies, game and rumpsteak pies, muffins, toast...

And this is without such well-known morning delicacies as devilled kidneys, kippers, bloaters, kedgeree, porridge, laver bread and so on. I am often tempted, when offered a 'full English breakfast', to request half a dozen of such items. While we are about it, the very word 'breakfast', which means literally and originally the first meal of the day, has been subverted to mean a single dish, so that one can get an 'all-day breakfast' – even in the form of a sandwich which includes bacon and egg.

Good English food?

Today's breakfast three times a day would no doubt leave one satisfied, if bored. On the other hand, the rest of English eating has been unfairly denigrated. It is true that there have been times when it has been poor. The restrictions of the two World Wars, and of post-war austerity, gave us a very limited cuisine, though actually quite a healthy one as we can now see. School and other institutional meals, too, have often been something of a horror story. And domestic cooking has too often lacked the basic skills of many other nations.

But there has always been good food if one knew where to find it, often in modest circumstances such as tea-rooms or bed-and-breakfast establishments. The much derided Women's Institutes and similar bodies have boasted excellent and dedicated cooks among their membership. London, and some other cities, have always had a rich variety of food, often supplied by immigrant cultures. More recently of course London has become one of the world's gastronomic centres, though often at remarkable prices. A great-aunt of mine, who was a nurse in London at the turn of the nineteenth century, could get the 'ordinary', as it had been called since Shakespeare's day, a decent three course dinner, for eighteen pence – $7^{1}/2$p. The equivalent would cost £30 or £40 today.

The vast increase in travel has made many aware of the falsity of foreign stereotypes, including that of the meagre continental breakfast. Of course there is the 'café complet' for those who wish it. And there are also mass holiday resorts which seek to supply what their visitors are, no doubt correctly, supposed to want – fry-ups, with plenty of ketchup. But half-way decent establishments all over Europe offer breakfasts that put ours to shame, often of a cold buffet type, with a choice of many sorts of bread, rolls, biscuits, meat and cheeses, eggs, fish, patés and what have you. I've sometimes thought, if you want to eat well in (say) Norway, you should take breakfast once a day – you won't need much else.

7

CHILD PRODIGIES COME TO NO GOOD END
They 'burn out' – 'early ripe, early rot'.

It is easy to find examples of brilliant children who have failed to fulfill their apparent potential. One of the most famous in his day was William James Sidis (1898-1944). Undoubtedly extremely gifted, he was 'hot-housed' by his eccentric father Dr Boris Sidis. At nine he qualified to enter Harvard, but was thought too young and had to wait until he was eleven. But he later achieved little of note. And when such a sad case occurs, the press seldom fails to draw a general lesson from it. Lena Zavaroni, who was a star as a child singer in the 1970s, by the age of 34 was living on benefit. She died in 1999. *The Times* (13th March 1998) remarked: 'For every well-adjusted, grown-up and happy former child star, there's someone whose life has been blighted'. At least this makes it fifty-fifty.

Life-long success

It is just as easy to find examples of early excellence followed by later success. The one that comes to everyone's mind is Wolfgang Amadeus Mozart (1756-1791) who played the harpsichord at three, and at five composed and gave his first public performance. His whole career, until his tragically early death, was one of artistic if not financial triumph. Less well known but more recent, the pianist Mieczyslaw Horszowski appeared in public at seven, and was still doing so successfully *ninety* years later. He died in 1993, aged 101. Indeed perhaps the majority of outstanding musicians have shown early talent. And in chess, another rich field for exceptional early talent, it has been claimed that of all those who might merit the title 'prodigy', only one, Pomar, failed to reach their potential – he became 'only' a moderate grandmaster.

Actually there is no precise definition of 'child prodigy'. Achieving a first class degree in mathematics at, say, twenty-one, would hardly count, although it is far beyond the ability of all but a few. But at thirteen, as Ganesh Sittampalam did in 1992, one can hardly withhold the title. He seems to have taken it in his stride and went on to take a D.Phil at Oxford and become a successful researcher. His friendly web-site makes no mention of the degree that put him in all the papers and on many television programmes. Balamurali Ambati, at thirteen, declared he wanted to be the world's youngest doctor, and qualified M.D. four years later. He now specialises in ophthalmology.

Boy film stars

What we want in order to test the popular idea is data, but it is hard to come by. Exceptional children often appear in the press, in fact about every ten days or so on average, as I know from a ten-year pursuit of them. But most of them then disappear from the public eye. One does not know if they become successful, even famous in their own field, or just get by, or fail miserably. One group I've looked at is boy film actors, mainly based on the first attempt to collect details of a really large number of them, over 2000 (*The Moving Picture Boy* by J. Holmstrom, published by Michael Russell, 1998). He gives the subsequent careers of only some, but from this sample, supplemented by other sources, I found that about 40% could be said to have had good or excellent careers, about 50% average and only 8% definitely poor or failure. About half stayed in acting, a quarter remained in show business in some capacity, and the other quarter went into something quite different. The most famous of all child film stars in her day, Shirley Temple, continued acting into her twenties but eventually became a successful diplomat.

This is pretty consistent with the details I have compiled over many years on exceptional achievement in childhood. Most gifted children do well in later life, though not necessarily as brilliantly as in earlier years. Conversely most, though not all, outstanding adults have shown ability when young. Those who have performed consistently at the highest level, like Mozart, are rare. Most careers have a peak, which may last a very short or a quite long time, and many factors contribute to this besides sheer talent. At any rate, I have no hesitation in dismissing the gloomy prognostications that so often accompany stories of extraordinary children.

8

COLUMBUS DISCOVERED AMERICA
It depends on what you mean by 'discovered'. And by 'America'. And if he didn't, who did?

Christopher Columbus (1451-1506) did of course sail across the Atlantic Ocean in 1492. His aim was to find a route to China that might be quicker and easier than round the southern end of Africa and then across the Indian Ocean. Trade with the Far East was a lucrative enterprise. Columbus, a native of Genoa, which was a thriving port, went to sea in his teens and became an experienced navigator. Around 1471 he put his idea to the King of Portugal, but failed to convince him. About 1485 he tried again, in Spain, where he got the support of two influential priests, one being the Royal Treasurer and the other the Bishop of Placencia. But King Ferdinand was preoccupied with the final stages of his campaign to drive the Moors out of Spain, and again the plan was rejected. Columbus approached both Charles VIII of France, and Henry VII of England. Charles was involved in wars in Italy, and Henry was cautious and frugal. Finally in 1491, with the fall of Granada,

Ferdinand was ready for another venture. Columbus sailed on 3rd August 1492.

Reaching America

On the morning of 12th October Columbus landed on what is now Watling's Island, Bahamas, and claimed it for the King of Spain. Of course there were people already there, but they were obviously uncivilised and non-Christian and so they didn't really count. Columbus made three further voyages across the Atlantic. On the first he reached what are now Dominica, Jamaica, Haiti and Cuba. On the second he reached Honduras, and on the last Trinidad and the mainland of America, near the mouth of the Orinoco River. He knew that his original landfall had proved to be an island, and believed to the end that only islands lay between him and the ultimate goal, with the Indian Ocean just beyond the points he had reached. Thus, it is a nice question whether he can be said to have discovered, or merely reached, America.

And, of course, he had had predecessors. Long before, perhaps as long as twenty-five thousand years before, though some estimates are smaller, human beings had crossed what was then a land bridge across the Bering Straits to Alaska. *H. sapiens sapiens*, wandering slowly out of central Africa, wound their way across Asia and into the Americas, and eventually down to the very southern end, Tierra del Fuego. On the way they created many and various societies and remarkable civilisations including the Aztec and the Inca. All, however, succumbed to the Europeans who followed in the wake of Columbus. Today a last few native peoples are clinging precariously on to their ancient way of life in South America, while others have adapted more or less successfully to modern ways. Their ancestors could be said to have first claim to have 'discovered' America.

The next claimant, chronologically, would seem to be the prophet Lehi. According to the Church of Jesus Christ of Latter Day Saints, better known as Mormons, about 600 BCE he led a group of Hebrews to America, where they created an advanced civilisation. As, however, no trace of this has ever been discovered, and it rests entirely on the revelations afforded to the founding prophet of the church, Joseph Smith, it can perhaps be set aside. A better claim has recently been made for Polynesian voyagers, perhaps from Hawaii, making landfall on the coast of California, possibly as long as 1,500 years ago. It remains speculative but is by no means impossible in principle, given the known seafaring skills of these people.

Vikings and Chinese

The record of Vikings reaching America is increasingly well established. There was, it is true, a hooha about the so-called Vinland Map, supposedly from the fifteenth century and showing a Viking view of the coast of North America. Published in 1965, it seems generally agreed to be a fake. Better evidence comes from the Viking Sagas and from archaeology. In the 1960s evidence was found of what seems to have been a short-lived settlement around 1000 CE, at Epaves Bay in Newfoundland.

The Sagas are epic accounts of Viking adventures which have proved to be generally reliable as history, as far as they can be checked. Two of them, the Greenlanders' Saga and Eirik's Saga, tell of what we would call America. It seems that about 955 CE one Bjarni Harjolfsson sighted land, but did not land himself. But Leif Erikson, known as Leif the Lucky, did so. And Thorfinn Karlsefni, an Icelandic trader, did as well, and with companions stayed for three years. His son, Snorri, was born there, and was three when they left. It seems that hard winters, and hostility from natives, caused them to abandon the adventure. Remarkably, Thorfinn's wife, Glaumbaer, later in life made a pilgrimage from Iceland to Rome, surely one of the most extraordinary stories of travel ever.

There is yet another claim. Between 1405 and 1433 the Chinese admiral Zheng He (it is also transliterated as Cheng Ho, and pronounced something like 'jung hu'), made a series of remarkable voyages at the command of the Emperor. Designated Admiral of the Western Seas, he reached India, Sri Lanka, Indonesia, the Philippines and Malaysia. The story is told by Louise Levathes in *When China Ruled the Seas*, reprinted 1996. It seems that Chinese shipwrights created ocean-going vessels, vast for the time, some several hundred feet in length, when Columbus's flagship the Santa Maria was well short of one hundred. Zheng He's fleets were numerous and so were his crews, and his voyages were successful.

But a change of regime brought a change of policy. With an inward-looking emphasis on central control which has dominated much of China's history for more than two thousand years, the construction of ocean-going vessels was forbidden, and Zheng He's ships and records destroyed.

However in 2002 a former naval officer, Commander Gavin Menzies, advanced the claim that Zheng He had actually reached not only the Caribbean but also the west coast of America, and indeed had circumnavigated the world. It is all described in his book *The Year China Discovered the World*, i.e. 1421. Commander Menzies was naturally delighted when in 2006 Liu Gang, a Chinese lawyer, produced a remarkably accurate map of the world dated 1418, correctly showing North America. This has yet to be authenticated.

These events include some of the great might-have-beens of history. What if Zheng He had colonised America? Actually the Chinese have not, historically, been colonisers, but what if his voyages had not been cut short and China had become a great maritime power, before Spain, Portugal and Britain got going? What if Thorfinn Karlsefni had stuck it out, and been followed by others? What if Columbus had convinced Henry VII and not King Ferdinand? What, indeed, if the Bering Straits had proved a bridge too far, before rising sea levels made a land passage impassable? I leave it to you.

9

ALEISTER CROWLEY WAS THE WICKEDEST MAN IN THE WORLD

The 'Great Beast 666', black magician, Satanist and perpetrator of unknown horrors and especially sexual perversions.

There are perhaps two sets of people who may not agree with this. The first is those who respect Crowley as a great magical adept, the other is those who have never, or only vaguely, heard of him. He was for a time famous or notorious, seldom out of the headlines. The label 'the wickedest man in the world' was a newspaper gimmick, which appeared in the down-market, one might say bottom of the market, journal *John Bull*. That and the *Sunday Express* got acres of copy out of Crowley's real or alleged iniquities. Crowley himself was never averse to fame, or notoriety. He had a posthumous revival of both when his face appeared on the cover of the Beatles's smash hit *Sergeant Pepper's Lonely Hearts Club Band* in 1967.

Magic

Aleister (his own choice of name, replacing his original Edward Alexander) Crowley (1875-1947) was born in ultra-respectable Leamington Spa to well-off parents who belonged to the fundamentalist, sternly moralistic, sect the Plymouth Brethren. He had an unhappy childhood at home (his mother called him 'the beast'), and at a succession of schools. He excelled only at mountaineering and chess. He gained a place at Cambridge, but did not graduate. He did, however, get to know quite a lot of subsequently famous people; and he became fascinated by systems of magic, and all sorts of ancient, or supposedly ancient, esoteric knowledge and rituals.

In the late nineteenth century there was a surge of interest in these, in particular in a group known now as the magicians of the Golden Dawn. The Hermetic Order of the Golden Dawn, supposedly ancient, seems to have been the invention of a London coroner, Dr William Wynn Westcott. It was enthusiastically taken up by others who created a complex set of rules and rituals, partly invented and partly derived from accounts of former magical or mystical orders, such as Rosicrucians and Masons. Into this order Crowley was inducted at age twenty-three, and he rapidly rose through the ranks. Fairly soon, however, he quarrelled with most of the leaders, to whom he considered himself far superior. He developed his own systems, again partly out of his own imagination and partly from what became a really extensive knowledge of esoteric beliefs and of non-Christian religions.

The Book of the Law

Things came to a head in Cairo in 1904. In the course of various magical practices Crowley, according to his own account, became the recipient of messages from a supernatural being named Aiwass (to his critics, Eyewash), who stood behind him and dictated. The result was *The Book of the Law*. As very often happens with such messages, Crowley was certain that the source was external to himself, and it was not only unexpected but unwelcome.

The main principle of the Book was one for which he was frequently pilloried, *'Do what thou wilt shall be the whole of the Law'*. Defenders are quick to point out, correctly, that this does not mean, remove all constraints on behaviour. The injunction means, to become aware of what is one's true nature. Crowley's magic, like other such systems, is essentially concerned, both with bringing about changes in accordance with the will (sometimes given as a definition of magic), and with individual spiritual or psychological development.

However, Crowley's conception of such development, and still more his means, were what got him into trouble. As many religions have done, he used a wide range of drugs, which were then freely available – marijuana, cocaine, opium, alcohol, heroin. To the last he became addicted for the rest of his life. His view had been that addiction was a mental matter, to which he could rise superior. Indeed a belief in the powers of his own mind was one of his most dominant traits. He sincerely thought he was the greatest living poet, though his mass of verse seems to most critics worthless. Similarly his continued progression through the magical ranks, now largely invented by himself, led him at last to claim the degree of *Ipsissimus*, equivalent to a deity.

Far more newsworthy was his sexual life. Continually promiscuous in his private life, he also incorporated sex acts with both men and women into his magical rituals, again drawing on various ancient traditions. It may be too facile to see all this as an over-reaction to the harsh rules of his childhood, just as he rejected the name his parents had given him. But certainly he threw out all the sexual taboos of a rigid Christianity – far more sensational behaviour in his day than ours.

Decline and fall

Two episodes especially marred his reputation. He spent the first World War safely in America, where he vociferously advocated the German cause. He later implausibly claimed he was trying to discredit it, by exaggerating it. After the war he set up what would now be called, perhaps, a hippy commune, in Sicily, dignified by the title of the Abbey of Thelema, in fact a small and insanitary cottage. Sex and drugs, and the unrelated death of one member, made it notorious. After a couple of years it was ended by the Italian authorities, largely in a campaign against secret movements. Crowley's last decades were downhill, increasingly frail, drug addicted, bankrupt, he survived on writing, some money from another marriage, and contributions from followers. He died in the seaside resort of Hastings, as inappropriately respectable as his birthplace.

Crowley seems a kind of psychopathic personality, reckless of his own fate or of his effects on others – wives, lovers and followers were often treated with careless cruelty. Two committed suicide. But although he went to extremes in these various ways, most of his behaviour can be readily paralleled. Drugs and sexual promiscuity are hardly rare, nor are delusions of grandeur. Crowley can hardly be said to have contributed anything positive to the human race, unless one believes in his magical systems. And he behaved badly to quite a few individuals. But to call him the wickedest man in the world, in a century which gave us Hitler, Stalin, Pol Pot, Mao Tse Tung, Saddam Hussein and others responsible for the death and suffering of many millions, makes sense only in journals whose circulation depends on a nasty diet of 'shock horror' titillation.

The complex story is unravelled in *The Magicians of the Golden Dawn* by Ellic Howe, 1972, and *Aleister Crowley: The Beast Demystified* by Roger Hutchinson, 1998, among others.

THE *CUTTY SARK* WAS THE FASTEST OF THE CLIPPER SHIPS

which were built to get the new crop of tea each year from China back to Britain as quickly as possible.

The *Cutty Sark* lies in dry dock at Greenwich, a popular tourist attraction and a romantic sight. She is the only remaining complete example of the great 'tea clippers' of the second half of the nineteenth century. She is gradually falling to pieces for want of funds to keep her in repair, though recently (2005), more money has been announced. Within sight of her, the empty Millennium Dome, a large tent, has been using up £250,000 per month of public money in upkeep, despite having been 'sold', effectively given away, for commercial use. But that I suppose is politics.

The tea-clippers
Anyhow, the 'clippers' were the culmination of the tradition of sailing ships going back well into prehistory. There have been faster sailing vessels built since, but only for racing. The clippers

were working ships, built to make speed in any conditions and through the roughest seas, with a valuable and perishable cargo. They were also perhaps the most beautiful ships ever created. Even now the *Cutty Sark*, shorn of her sails and sequestered from wind and waves, makes an irresistible impression. Magnificent as she must have been, however, she was probably not the fastest of all.

The era of the clipper ships was a relatively short one. In 1842 the first Opium War ended with the Treaty of Nanking. The war was fought primarily so that British merchants could continue exporting opium from India to the lucrative Chinese market, despite it having been made illegal by the Chinese government in 1800. It was one of the more indefensible actions of the British Empire. However, it resulted in Hong Kong being ceded to Britain, and the creation of five open ports – Canton, Shanghai, Foochow, Ningpo and Amoy. From these tea was exported. High prices could be got for the first of the new crop, and hence the clippers. Advances in design and materials made them the finest sailing ships ever built. But the introduction of steam, and in particular the opening of the Suez Canal in 1869, eventually made them obsolete. Their prime was thus about twenty-five years.

The *Cutty Sark* twice made a trip from a Chinese port to London in 110 days, certainly among the fastest. But exact comparisons are impossible. It was not a controlled race. Ships left when they were loaded, subject to wind and tides. Different routes might be taken, according to the judgement of the captain. Some would take a shorter but riskier way, others longer but safer. Some would be more successful at predicting wind and weather. In some cases, accidents supervened, as in 1872, when the *Cutty Sark*, competing against the *Thermopylae*, lost her rudder. (The latter is sometimes said to have been American, but she was from Aberdeen.).

Captain Shewan

We have to turn to the opinions of the men who knew the ships at first hand. To my mind the most convincing account is that of Captain Andrew Shewan, in his book *The Great Days of Sail* (1927). He went to sea in 1863 and commanded tea clippers, his first in 1872 at only 23, as his father had before him. He knew all the great ships and sailed in or against many of them. His considered judgement was that the *Ariel*, built in 1865 by Steele's of Greenock, was the fastest of all. She was not suited to all conditions and could become dangerous in heavy seas, which may explain the fact that she was lost without trace in 1872. But in good conditions she could outsail anything afloat. Shewan also thought her the most beautiful. After her, he names the *Titania*, *Thermopylae*, *Cutty Sark*, *Spindrift* and *Leander* 'with very little to choose between any of them'.

The *Cutty Sark* was built in 1869 in Dumbarton. She was best in strong winds, and several records are attributed to her, though there was no exact record-keeping, and Captain Shewan thinks them exaggerated. When the tea trade declined, the *Cutty Sark* was used for iron and wool to and from Australia. In 1916 she was dismasted, was sold, re-rigged, and re-named. In 1922 she was sold again and used as a stationary training ship, until her installation at Greenwich in 1949. 'Sark' means a shirt in Scots dialect, and her figurehead clutches a tattered piece of cloth. See her if you can.

11

CHARLES DARWIN INVENTED THE THEORY OF EVOLUTION
And it's only a theory after all, isn't it?

Charles Darwin (1809-1882) is perhaps the best known of the three men who in the nineteenth century fundamentally altered the way we think about ourselves as a species, and our place in nature. The others were Sigmund Freud and, least generally known, Francis Galton. Like most innovators, all drew on existing ideas, but produced a new and convincing synthesis, with far-reaching implications. Darwin did not invent evolution. He did not even discover it. What he did was show how it could work, and how it could put order into a mass of observed facts.

Evolution
The idea that existing species had developed gradually from primitive forms is at least as old as classical Greece, and was

42

discussed by Aristotle (384-322 BCE). This idea never disappeared from Western thought, but it was in disfavour with the dominant Christian Church, which for centuries held that every species was created by God and was immutable. In the seventeenth and eighteenth centuries new evidence stirred controversy over the issue. Fossils of animals which evidently no longer existed became increasingly known, suggesting that species could at least die out – and presumably be replaced by others. Curiously enough, the Darwin family hailed from the village of Elston, where in 1719 the first recognised fossil bones of a giant reptile were discovered. Practical husbandry developed more systematic breeding programmes of domestic animals, showing that species could change. Geologists such as Charles Lyell (1797-1875) showed convincingly that the earth must be far older than the age implied by the Book of Genesis. Archbishop Ussher had famously calculated that it was created on 23rd October 4004 BC. On the other hand, the success of Carl Linnaeus (1707-1778) in developing a system of biological classification tended to support fixity of species.

Erasmus Darwin

But evolution was in the air. Darwin's grandfather, Dr Erasmus Darwin (1731-1802), one of the group of speculative thinkers and inventors who formed the famous Lunar Society of Birmingham, so called because they met when the moon gave enough light to see them safely home after meetings, was an evolutionist. He cared little for received opinion or for the Church. He pointed, first, to those animals that change greatly during their life cycle, such as butterflies. Second, there were those that had produced many varieties over long periods of time, either by chance or by breeding, such as dogs, cattle and sheep. Third, there were sports or freaks, including those he had seen himself such as 'a breed of cats with an additional claw on every foot'.

Dr Darwin argued that all animals 'undergo perpetual transformations', under the influence of three impulses, those of sex, hunger and security. Those individuals most successful at mating, feeding, and surviving danger, will be those that propagate the species – 'survival of the fittest' in a later phrase. And they will transmit those characteristics which have made them successful, under varying conditions – speed for pursuit or escape, claws or beaks for different foods, and so on.

The Theory
Charles Darwin, for his part, was fascinated, as is well known, by the variety of species he saw when sailing as unpaid naturalist on *HMS Beagle* in 1831-36. The famous example is the finches on the Galapagos Islands, which seemed to have developed along different lines from finches elsewhere. An idea of how this might come about was suggested by the work of the Rev Thomas Malthus (1766-1834) on the struggle for existence in human populations. The key to evolution, Darwin argued, was chance variation coupled with natural selection. He did not, of course, know what the mechanism of variation was, namely genetics, but whatever it was, it produced in each generation small differences, some of which were more conducive to survival and so to offspring. And that, in essence, is what has proved to be the case.

It is necessary to explain that it is the 'Theory of Evolution' not because it is speculative, as one might say one has a theory that it always rains on Bank Holidays. A scientific theory is an ordered, systematic presentation of observations that makes them explicable, and which yields testable hypotheses. Or as the Random House *American College Dictionary* has it, 'a coherent group of general propositions used as principles of explanation for a class of phenomena'. The Theory was at first opposed by some, on both religious and scientific grounds, but was eventually accepted, and is so today by, effectively, all informed people. Evolution itself is an observed fact. The details of how it works are still being explored, not least through advances in genetics.

In some quarters, however, it is controversial or even denied. This came to public attention with the 'Scopes trial' in Dayton, Tennessee in 1925, when a school teacher was condemned for teaching a non-Biblical account of creation. Recently, a revival of Christian fundamentalism has strenuously urged that so-called 'creation science' should be taught alongside, or even instead of, evolutionary theory. It should hardly be necessary to say that there is simply no evidence at all for the 'creation' view, which is not science at all but a religious myth, one of the vast number of fanciful accounts of how we and the world were made, that cultures have produced in the absence of any firm knowledge. Christians are not able to show why theirs is to be preferred, and of course only some take the Genesis account literally, others treating it as a metaphor or fable. The hardliners rely on a combination of ignorance, distortion, fabrication and fallacious reasoning. But to illustrate all these would fill too many pages that can be better employed. Numerous websites can be consulted – to name just two: www.ucmp.berkeley.edu/history/evolution and www.talkorigins.org.

12

DICK TURPIN RODE TO YORK

on his famous mare Black Bess, although precisely where from, and when, and why, very few people can tell you.

There seems to be a general idea that it was from London, and that it may have been something to do with establishing an alibi, although against that, there are numerous places claiming to have been on his itinerary, and where he stopped, or slept, or ate, which can only with the help of a strong imagination, and a weak grasp of geography, be said to be on the road from London to York.

In fact this one seems to be fairly well established, both as to what actually happened, and as to how it became a legend.

Turpin, petty criminal

Richard Turpin was born in Essex, probably at either Thaxted or Hempstead, in 1706. He was apprenticed to a butcher, but fairly soon turned to petty crime – robbery and smuggling. With others of the same inclination, who became known as the Essex Gang, he specialised in terrorising, torturing and robbing the female residents of lonely farmhouses. Other crimes, including cattle stealing, highway robbery and murder, were all grist to their mill. By 1736 he merited a bounty of £50 for his capture, increased to £100 the following year (a man could live for a year on that). He then made his way to York, where for a time he passed as a respectable citizen under the name of John Palmer or Parmen. Actually he continued his career of robbery, mostly some distance away in Lincolnshire. Eventually apprehended, he was convicted on two counts, sentenced to death, and hanged at what is now York racecourse, in April 1739.

On the scaffold Turpin put on a show of nonchalant defiance, and perhaps due to this was soon, like many others of his kind, celebrated in song, the mass media of the day, as 'brave Turpin hero'. Around 1800, written accounts began to include the story of the ride to York. Such a ride had actually been made, back in 1676, by one John 'Nick' Nevison, from Gads Hill in Kent – 190 miles in fifteen hours. It was indeed to establish an alibi, and for it he became known as 'Swift Nick'. This story became attached to the later man. Turpin might nevertheless have sunk into well-deserved obscurity but for a popular novel entitled Rookwood, published by W. Harrison Ainsworth in 1834. He gave Dick Turpin a minor role, but included the ride. Ainsworth had Turpin start from Westminster, however; and it seems to be he who invented 'Black Bess'.

Romanticised villains
Turpin seems to have been a thoroughly nasty bit of work – no knight of the road he – and ended regretted by few. But he has become romanticised in a way that villains frequently are, and not only those with the glamour of history about them. Reginald (Reggie) Kray died in 2000. His funeral cortege through the East End of London was reported as two miles long. When not in prison, Reggie and his twin brother Ronald spent nearly all their lives in petty but often violent crime, apart from a period early on when they were moderately successful professional boxers. They

were called up for National Service in 1951 but deserted (as their father had before them). They cannot be said to have contributed anything whatever to society. On the contrary, they (and their elder brother Charlie) cost us all a considerable amount, in clearing up after their crimes, convicting them, and maintaining them in prison. But they have become almost folk heroes, aided partly by their lower class origins and their dislike of those born better off, and partly by a fictionalised version of their lives in the film *The Krays* (1990) when they were portrayed by the glamorous rock stars Gary and Martin Kemp.

Turpin has been played on film by actors as various as Matheson Lang, Philip Friend, Richard O'Sullivan, Tom Mix and Sid James (*Carry On Dick!*), mostly as a kind of Robin Hood, charming rogue type of fellow. Dick Turpin rides on, probably the only highwayman whose name is still known to the public. (The whole story has been explored by James Sharpe in *Dick Turpin: The Myth of the English Highwayman*, 2004)

13

SIR FRANCIS DRAKE DEFEATED THE SPANISH ARMADA

after finishing his game of bowls on Plymouth Hoe

The story of the bowls may be true, although it is not recorded in print until 1624. Drake was the sort of man to have said 'There is time to finish the game, and beat the Spanish too', or something like it, as he allegedly did. The Hoe, of course, is a grassy headland above Plymouth Harbour, where in July 1588 the English fleet was waiting for news of a sighting of the Spanish invasion. When it came, the English ships were stuck there for some hours due to the state of wind and tides. So there was perforce a delay, and time for a game.

Drake the adventurer

Drake was one of the most extraordinary adventurers in an age of adventurers. His voyage round the world in 1577-1580 was the first by an Englishman, and when one sees the sort of tub in which these early voyages were made, one is astonished that anyone got further from England than France. (There is a replica of Drake's

Golden Hinde at Southwark.) He was also a renowned and feared warrior, in the style of the time half privateer, half patriot. But he was never in command of the English fleet. When the Spanish invasion threatened, that honour was give to Lord Howard of Effingham, as Lord Admiral. Drake was made Vice-Admiral.

The threat had been building for many years. It is a complex story, but the essential causes were religious and political. Philip II of Spain was the ruler of a large part of Europe and, at least officially and by decision of the Pope, most of the Americas. He had recently gained control of Portugal, with its great maritime experience and resources. From America Spain obtained vast wealth in the form of gold and precious stones. This trade was the object of frequent plundering raids, not least by the English. Some were led by Drake himself, who had also attacked Spanish ships in their very own harbours – 'singeing the King of Spain's beard' at Cadiz in 1587. Coupled with the devious diplomacy of Queen Elizabeth I, England varied from being a nuisance to a positive danger. Philip was also a religious fanatic, a leader of the Counter-Reformation campaign to reinstate Roman Catholicism as the one true faith. Indeed this may well have been his major motivation to undertake the 'Enterprise of England'.

The Enterprise of England

However this may be, Philip finally determined on an invasion of England. The plan was to send a vast fleet to command the Channel, so that an army could be transported across it from the Continent. This would be supplied by Philip's general the Duke of Parma, who was waging a continuous struggle against the Protestant Dutch. The well trained soldiers should easily overcome the English, who had no standing army and few defences on land. Lengthy preparations at last resulted in the assembly of the fleet, at Lisbon, some 130 ships of various types, and 19,000 men, both sailors and soldiers.

From that point on, one might say, from the Spanish point of view Sod's Law ruled. Practically everything that could go wrong, did. To begin with, the capable Admiral who was to have led the expedition, the Marquis de Santa Cruz, died suddenly. Philip's replacement was the Duke of Medina Sidonia, an able and faithful man who commanded respect as a senior aristocrat, but who lacked any experience of naval warfare. He was apparently wary of the whole undertaking, but Philip put his trust in God, who could not fail to ensure victory for the faith.

However, after one or two mishaps the fleet, probably the largest naval force ever assembled up to then, reached sight of England in good order. There is some argument as to whether it could have successfully attacked the English in Plymouth Harbour, and whether the decision not to do so was due to the strict instructions of the King to carry on to the rendezvous. Philip was a man who wished to control every detail in person. Of course there was no way of communicating with the fleet at sea, nor of it doing so with Parma.

In any case, the English fleet got out of harbour, and gained the weather gauge, that is behind the Spanish with the wind from the rear. Thus they could attack or retreat at will. They were also faster and more manoeuverable than the Spanish ships. The Spanish method of fighting was to close with an enemy vessel, fire one massive broadside, then board her. The English were trained and equipped to fire and reload rapidly, and to stand off rather than board.

In the first engagement one ship, the *Nuestra Senora del Rosario*, was disabled and fell behind. Drake, true to his privateering past, broke ranks to capture her – to say nothing of 55,000 gold ducats, as she turned out to be one of the fleets' pay ships (about £15,000, when Drake's pay as Vice-Admiral was about £500 a year). Drake later claimed he came up with her by chance, but it remains a possible criticism. Well, of course the planned Spanish rendezvous failed. Even when communications were possible, what had been overlooked was that the Spanish ships were too large to approach the shallow shores where Parma waited, while his troops, in barges, could not be sent out for fear of attack by shallow-draught Dutch 'fly-boats'.

End of the Armada

Off Calais, the English employed fireships to break up the Spanish fleet. Although they survived this fairly well, the subsequent battle of Gravelines (in which Drake played a major part), although inconclusive, finally put paid to any chance of an invasion. Prevailing winds and English ships made a return through the Channel impossible, and Medina Sidonia set out for home around the stormy north coast of the British Isles. Remarkably, about half his fleet eventually made it.

Drake didn't defeat the Armada, though he had a vital role. He is of course far more famous than his official commander, Lord Howard. He symbolises not only an age of adventure, but the point at which England, and later Britain, began her rise to world power. Similarly the defeat of the Armada has come to be seen as one of those defining moments of an emerging nation, often of a David-and-Goliath type, like the Greek defeat of the Persian invasion at Marathon, and, ironically perhaps, the American defeat of the British in the War of Independence.

14

DRUIDS BUILT STONEHENGE

**Or at any rate they have some ancient connection with it, which
is why they gather there at the summer solstice.**

There are two disjunctions here. The original Druids had nothing
to do with Stonehenge, or other megalithic monuments. And the
various groups of Druids today have almost no connection with
the ancient ones. Stonehenge is the most famous and impressive
of a large number of 'henges', some of wood, and related
monuments such as standing stones, stone circles, and
earthworks, built in Britain and elsewhere some three to six
thousand years ago.

Stonehenge itself was constructed in a whole series of stages
between about 3500 and 1500 BCE (Before the Common Era, the
religiously neutral version of Before Christ). Much modern
research has gone into showing that it, and other structures, could
have had astronomical functions. The fact is that we have no
certain idea how they were used, and can only guess at some
combination of astronomical, religious, magical or ceremonial
purposes. No new structures were built after about 1400 BCE.

The Druids

The original Druids were a part of the Celtic cultures which were widely spread across Europe in the late Bronze Age. In the eighth to sixth centuries BCE they reached Britain, while around 400 they pushed into northern Italy, and in 390 sacked Rome. Earlier histories tell their story as conquests by a fairly homogeneous people, spreading out from their central European homelands to occupy territory from Ireland to beyond the Black Sea, but eventually being displaced, in the West, in their turn by Germanic peoples, following the end of the Roman Empire around 400 CE. In Britain they were thus reduced to the western fringes, Wales, Cornwall and Ireland. Scotland was colonised from Ireland. More recent accounts stress rather the diversity of the Celtic peoples and cultures, and a spread by gradual transmission of cultural practices rather than by conquest or invasion.

We actually know very little about the Druids, though quite a lot about the Celts. There are three main sources of information. First there are accounts by classical writers, of which the fullest and perhaps best is that of Julius Caesar, whose knowledge came from his campaigns in Gaul in 58 to 50 BCE. Second are the much later traditional practices and records in Wales and especially Ireland, where Celtic culture survived longest, at least in some form. And third there is archaeology. The classical accounts suffer from being in general hostile, and from a tendency to see any other culture as primitive, and at the same time to interpret it in terms of their own. The Irish writings date from the twelfth century, though these derive from earlier sources, perhaps before the fifth century, that is pre-Christian. The Welsh documents are later and thoroughly Christianised.

Archaeological evidence is rather slim. The Celts were not builders in stone though they did leave many smaller artifacts. From all this we can more or less infer that the Druids were a recognised elite and trained class in Celtic societies, whose functions can perhaps be summarised as those of 'wise men', experts in traditional lore and practices. Both classical and Irish sources describe three elite orders, Druids, bards (poets and singers), and seers (prophets and diviners). Religion included numerous gods and goddesses, some purely local. Sacrifice, perhaps including human, accompanied divination. Some kind of cult of the human head included collecting the heads of enemies slain in battle. Trees, groves and forests were sacred, especially the oak, ash, yew and hazel, as was water. The number three had particular significance. Whatever the Druids did or believed, they diminished under Roman rule, and disappeared with the advent of Christianity. By the eighth century only the Greek and Latin accounts remained.

Modern Druids

Modern Druids emerged a thousand years later. John Aubrey (1626-1697) speculated that stone circles were Druid temples. The specific association with Stonehenge comes initially from the pioneering antiquary William Stukeley (1678-1765). He explored and recorded many ancient monuments, especially Avebury and Stonehenge, which he described as 'A Temple of the British Druids'. For him the Druids became philosopher-priests, possessors of ancient wisdom, who championed liberty against Rome. His enthusiasm gained him the nick-name of 'the Arch-Druid'.

The eighteenth century was a period of the unification of Britain, with the Act of Union of 1707 ending the existence of Scotland as a separate state, the defeat of the Stuart monarchy in 1745, and the formal annexation of Ireland in 1801. At least partly as a reaction, there was an upsurge of interest in the Celts. In 1707 Edward Lhuyd, Welsh scholar and patriot, published his research into what he correctly saw were the related ancient languages of Brittany, Cornwall, Ireland, Scotland and Wales. This was perhaps the initiation of a new sense of Celtic identity, itself part of the larger Romantic movement. In the 1760s James MacPherson published his poems supposedly by 'Ossian', an ancient bard. The Highlands and Islands became tourist attractions, visited even by Dr Johnson. The novels and poems of Sir Walter Scott (1771-1832) celebrated the ideal of the noble clansman, and George IV wore a kilt when he visited Scotland in 1822.

In this climate Edward Williams, or in his Welsh name Iolo Morgannweg, a collector of manuscripts, writer and poet, 'revived' a mediaeval Order of Bards, supposed to have belonged to

Druidical times. Bards had existed as a literary class around 1080 to 1350, with the practice of 'chairing' those who became masters. The first modern celebration, or *Gorsedd*, was held on Primrose Hill in London in 1792. The spot is still used by today's Druids. Welsh people in London revived the practice of *eisteddfodau*, literary competitions, in the 1790s. A little before this, Henry Hurle, a London carpenter and builder, founded his Ancient Order of Druids in 1781. This subsequently split in 1833, one part transforming itself into a Benefit Society which still exists under the same name. The current Order of Bards, Ovates and Druids claims descent from another part. Another current claim is that in 1717 John Toland, an eccentric philosopher and politician, convened representatives of ten existing Druid 'groves' and formed the Druid Circle of the Universal Ancient Bond, with modern descendants. Toland was certainly interested in Druids, and planned, but did not write, a history of them, but I have found no confirmation that he ever did anything more. (See *The Pagan Religions of the Ancient British Isles* by Ronald Hutton, 1991.)

There are currently numerous Druid groups, many recent. They have a range of beliefs and practices, often centred on the sacredness of nature, and stressing 'Celtic' virtues such as honour, loyalty, hospitality, honesty, justice and courage. Many see themselves as drawing on ancient traditions, but also as innovating and developing new ways of living, community, ritual and the arts. Like all religions, they take what they find good, and reject other aspects, for example, the idea that Druids practiced ritual killing. Some suggest that while Druids did not build Stonehenge, they may have preceded the Celts, and been involved in its later stages, or at any rate used it, and understood its astronomical significance.

15

ENGLISH BEER IS DRUNK WARM

Mostly by men with beards and beer bellies, who are probably also train spotters, or even the ultimate horror, Morris Dancers! And the beer is flat and cloudy as well.

There are of course many people who do not suffer under this delusion, especially the 75,000 members (2005) of the Campaign for Real Ale, CAMRA. But there are many who do, especially our transatlantic visitors. Even former Prime Minister John Major listed warm beer among the features making up the England he liked.

Beer and 'real ale'

There are also many individuals, and drinking establishments, that do not serve beer or other beverages as they should do, whether too warm or too cold. And further, many different styles of beer are made in England, and thus are technically English. What we are talking about is 'real ale', a perhaps unfortunate label for a particular group of beers that have their home in England, though they are made equally well in Wales, Scotland and Ireland, and indeed, to some extent in many other countries including the USA. Makers of other varieties of beer point out with some justice that all ales are 'real', if they are alcoholic liquids brewed from grain. Another common error is to use 'England' when 'Britain' would be correct.

These beers, then, are made from malted, that is germinated and heated, barley, by a process known as top fermenting – the yeast floats on the top. Hops are added mainly for flavour, though originally as a preservative. When bottled or put in casks, beer undergoes a secondary fermentation. It should be kept, and served, at 52 to 55 degrees Fahrenheit, 12 to 13 Celsius. If colder, the flavour cannot be appreciated. Most other beers in the world are varieties of lager, which is bottom fermented, and distinguished by maturing for a period at a low temperature – lager means 'store'. It is often served at about 40°F, though cans or bottles kept in ice may be even lower. In passing, ice seems to exert a kind of fascination even when quite inappropriate. I have been offered iced sherry! and once had an American visitor who wanted ice with a single malt whisky.

There are liquids on sale under the name of beer that do not appear to have any taste at all, and thus are not harmed however low the temperature. Some are even made from rice. In one of Kingsley Amis's novels a character thinks that if he were a brewer he would use as a slogan simply 'Bloggs's Beer – Makes You Drunk', and that about sums up the merits of these products. If that is all you want, don't bother with real English ale. But for those who are unacquainted with it but wish to try, don't assume that any pub at random will serve it, or even, if they do, that they will keep it correctly. Best to consult the *Good Beer Guide* published annually by CAMRA.

2,000 real ales

However, this is only the general outline. There are currently around 2,000 different 'real ales' brewed in Britain, with strengths varying from about three to about twelve per cent alcohol by volume. There is room for variation in serving according to type of beer and personal preference. Some very strong beers can be enjoyed, like port or sherry, at or near room temperature. This is itself a vague concept, and it has been pointed out that it originated before central heating made us used to being quite warm whatever the season. The average home or office temperature would be too great for good beer. On the other hand, some pubs have cooler, though not chilled, beers for warmer days. Real ale will normally have some sparkle, due to the secondary fermentation which creates carbon dioxide. When this is over, remaining yeast and protein drop to the bottom of the bottle or barrel, and the beer is ready to be served. Many bottled real ales must be kept for some days to allow for settling and then poured carefully in one go, leaving the sediment behind, though a few can be drunk with it. Thus, it should normally be neither warm, flat, nor cloudy.

Now as to the drinkers of real ale. I don't know of any statistical survey of the appearance or activities of real ale drinkers. Beer festivals and pubs seem to contain a very wide selection. I don't know about train spotters, but most Morris Dancers seem to like a pint or six. And while we're about it, Morris Dancing is an ancient and beautiful art and skill. Only in England, with our passion for denigrating and destroying everything fine that we create, would it get the bad press it does. Why do we recklessly destroy canals, railways, great houses (and good small ones), local markets, traditional music, the countryside, civil liberties, democratic government – but there I go into politics again. Sorry.

16

ESKIMOS HAVE INNUMERABLE WORDS FOR SNOW
ranging from three to 'hundreds'. Do they? And if so, so what?

This is one of those academic ideas that has escaped and run amok, like Freud's 'unconscious mind' and indeed like Mary Shelley's monster created by the young scientist Frankenstein (not, incidentally, either Doctor or Baron as he so often appears). It seems to have started with the anthropologist Franz Boas in 1911. He stated that the Eskimo language had four words for 'snow' (snow on the ground, falling snow, drifting snow and a snow drift). His argument was that languages have the words their speakers need. Languages don't restrict thought, because they will readily adapt to new needs.

Language and thought
The Eskimos reappeared in a 1940 paper by the linguist Benjamin Lee Whorf. He implies five words, but does not clearly state a number, or his sources. His argument, however, in his later book *Language Thought and Reality* (1956) was that 'language is not

merely a reproducing instrument for voicing ideas but rather is itself the shaper of ideas'. Ideas correspondingly vary, from slightly to greatly, between different languages. George Orwell used this idea in his horror story of future society, *1984*. 'Newspeak' controls thought by controlling the vocabulary, so that new and revolutionary ideas cannot emerge. Conversely, it has been suggested that the power of classical Greek thought, which in effect invented philosophy, science and history, owed much to the peculiar qualities of the Greek language – but there were many other factors also. What became known as the 'Whorfian hypothesis' became widespread through two popular textbooks, Roger Brown's *Words and Things* (1958) and Edward Hall's *The Silent Languages* (1959).

From there it became common property, although with much confusion as to what it meant. One offering, for example, in *The Straight Dope: A Compendium of Human Knowledge* (1984), was that Eskimos have only a limited environment to talk about, and so have to make up a lot of words to fill up their conversation – including nine for snow. There is even a spoof list of one hundred including such gems as *MacTla*, snowburgers; *penstla*, the idea of snow; and *ever-tla*, a spirit made from mashed fermented snow. More generally, the implication seems to be that it is rather clever of the otherwise 'primitive' Eskimos to have been so inventive.

Thought and languages

There are several difficulties with the original idea. One is that there is no one 'Eskimo' language. Experts distinguish two main groups, Inuit and Yupik, with dialects which some count as separate languages. Second, languages vary in the extent to which they are analytic (or analysing), or synthetic. That is, do they vary meaning by different combinations of words, or by altering the word itself? English is largely but not wholly analytic. 'House' has the plural 'houses', but varieties of house are expressed by adding other words, sometimes hyphenated – doss-house, public house, chapter-house, manor house. Eskimo languages are synthetic. Thus we must ask, not how many words, but how many roots there are which can be modified for different sorts of snow. One authoritative answer is that there are only two, at least in the West Greenlandic version, one for snow falling or in the air, and one for snow on the ground.

But however many roots, or separate words, there are, the question of the relationship of language and thought remains. One can certainly argue that English, with a vocabulary drawn from many languages, principally Germanic and Romance, can express subtle variations of meaning. 'Fatherly' is not quite the same as 'paternal' (both ultimately from the same Indo-European root). 'Mutton' is not the same as 'sheep', whereas 'mouton' in French is. But it is a leap to conclude that we think differently from French or German speakers (even if it seems instantly appealing to say that we do). Strings of experiments have tried to elucidate the matter, still not conclusively. A much cited example of linguistic relativity, again used by Boas, is the colour spectrum. Some African languages apparently divide it up, not into our violet, indigo, blue, green, yellow, orange and red, but into only four, or even two, parts (for example with one division in the middle of what we call yellow.) But it does not follow that speakers of such languages see the rainbow differently to us.

Linguistic tools

It can be said that plumbers, architects, carpenters, lawyers all have a vocabulary that non-specialists lack. A society with advanced technologies, sciences and arts, and many specialisms, may have a larger vocabulary over-all than a more homogeneous and 'simpler' one in which all individuals share much the same life. Conversely, though, non-technological societies have many words referring to things (such as plants or animals) or conditions, that do not exist in 'advanced' cultures, which thus have no words for them. (Often, of course, the latter borrow the original word, or some approximation to it, like tomato from *tomatl*. It is alleged that the word 'kangaroo' meant 'I don't understand', in reply to a white man's question, 'What's that?'). It is not the case that some languages can be said to be 'simpler' or more 'primitive' than others. All are highly complex means of expression, and linguists aver that all have the power to express what the speakers of each want to say. How they do it is less important.

However, just recently some experiments have supported Whorf's hypothesis, in part. Tarahumara, a language of northern Mexico, has one word to cover blue and green. And speakers do, apparently, see less difference between the two than do English speakers. Further experiments show that words can affect what we perceive, but only what is perceived on the right side of the brain, presumably because that side is more concerned with language than the left.

17

BEFORE COLUMBUS, EVERYONE THOUGHT THE EARTH WAS FLAT

and if you went too far you would fall off the edge.

Before fourteen hundred and ninety-two, when Columbus sailed the ocean blue, was also a long time before Dr Gallup started his polls. It really isn't possible to say what 'everyone' thought, even in the Western societies from which Columbus came, let alone the rest of the world. But it is certainly possible to show that the idea of a spherical earth had been around for many centuries.

Flat or round?

One can speculate that early humans, if they considered the matter, may have drawn the obvious conclusion that they lived on a more or less flat surface, bounded perhaps by distant mountains. Certainly the earliest societies that we consider as civilisations, by virtue of organised cities, codes of law, literacy, formal education and so on, around seven thousand years ago in the Middle East, held that the earth was flat, with the heavens arched overhead and the sun passing across each day.

In the seventh century BCE, in the Greek city of Miletus in Asia Minor, we find the origins of systematic speculation about the nature of the universe, and of ourselves and our place in it. The pre-Socratic thinkers, as they are collectively labelled, are known almost entirely through accounts of later writers, especially Aristotle (384-322). The first, Thales (640-545) seems to have accepted the traditional flat view. Anaximander (611-547) favoured a cylinder. Aristotle himself considered the earth to be a sphere. The reasoning was partly based on observation. For example, the case of a distant ship coming into view. It is the masts that appear first, then the hull, showing that the sea must be curved. Again, the moon, even when other than full, appears as a curved shape, suggesting it is a sphere. And if one body in space is so, why not all? There were also more mystical arguments, based on the idea of a sphere as the perfect shape. More practically, Eratosthenes (276-196) calculated the circumference (north to south) as approximately 25,000 miles, not far from today's figure of 24,859.82.

Roman thinkers too, such as Pliny the Elder (23-79 CE), he who perished when Vesuvius destroyed Pompeii, and Ptolemy of Alexandria (90-168), held that the earth was a sphere. Part of the argument for a general belief to the contrary is that it was maintained by Christian thinkers. But this is by no means completely the case. Even some of what we would now call fundamentalists accepted that the earth is round. For example, Tertullian (160-220), who based himself on irrational faith, and argued that the Bible contains all we need to know, nevertheless did not maintain that the earth was flat. Many others, however, did follow the Bible doctrine, which derived from the earlier civilisations. The main ground was that the Bible cannot be mistaken, but there were also objections to the idea of there being other lands on the opposite side to ourselves, since this would have made it unlikely that the Apostles could have gone there, whereas the New Testament states that they visited all lands. St Augustine shrewdly pointed out, however, that even if there were such continents, they might not be inhabited. Alternatively the other half might be all sea.

Mediaeval views

The spherical earth concept was never lost during the Middle Ages. The Venerable Bede (673-735), 'the father of English scholarship', accepted it from Pliny, and implies that it was widely held, but was not something that should worry the Church. Johannes de Sacrobosco, otherwise John of Holywood (1195-1256), wrote a treatise on *The Sphere* which remained a standard text until the fifteenth century. He accepted the 'ship' argument for a round earth. The astrolabe, a mediaeval instrument of astronomy and navigation, developed by the fifth century, depends on the principle that the earth is round. Geoffrey Chaucer (c.1340-1400), wrote an instructional book about it for the benefit of his son Lewis, and clearly assumes that the latter is familiar with a round earth. Dante (1265-1321) similarly believes his audience knows the earth is round.

It may be noted that mediaeval monarchs on ceremonial occasions, such as coronations, held as one symbol a spherical orb, signifying the earth. Our sovereigns still do, with the orb surmounted by a cross indicating God's rule over the whole world. Some mediaeval religious images show Christ holding a sphere. Before Columbus several European voyagers crossed the equator, and noted that the different view of the heavens indicated a round earth.

The inspiration behind Columbus's voyage was, of course, to find an alternative route to the East. The surprise, at least to the educated, was not that this was possible, but that there was such a large obstacle in the way. Another surprise, perhaps, is that despite the earth being circled, by ships and then planes and at last by satellites from which its shape can be recorded with great accuracy, nevertheless the idea of a flat earth has survived until very recently, and possibly does so still. Specifically, in 1848 Samuel Birley Rowbotham propounded it in a paper to the Royal Astronomical Society, and embarked on a life-long campaign to prove it, based on the Bible. In 1873 he founded the Universal Zetetic (inquiring) Society. This was revived as the Flat Earth Society by Samuel Shenton in the twentieth century, and carried on by Charles Johnson and his wife until his death in 2001.

18

GEORGE WASHINGTON, WHEN A BOY, CUT DOWN HIS FATHER'S CHERRY TREE

but then owned up to it, thus proving his suitability to become,
in due course, President of a great emerging nation, on
account of his transparent honesty. That might prove
less advantageous today.

The legend has been repeated for generations, I certainly read it as
a child. But it is one of the easiest to dispose of. It stems from one
book, and as far as can be established was entirely the invention
of the author. The book was a life of Washington, first published
in 1800, but in a revised edition which first included the cherry
tree, in 1806. The author was the Reverend Mason Locke Weems
(1759-1825).

The original story
In the original version, George at the age of six was given a hatchet
(you know, the way boys of six are given hatchets). Not

surprisingly he went about having a go at anything in sight, such as his mother's pea sticks. He didn't cut down the cherry tree, but damaged it severely. His father questioned everyone, finally coming to George.

'George', said his father, 'do you know who killed that beautiful little cherry tree yonder in the garden?'

This was a tough question, and George staggered under it for a moment, but quickly recovered himself; and looking at his father, with the sweet face of youth brightened with the inexpressible charm of all-conquering truth, he bravely cried out, 'I can't tell a lie, Pa, you know I can't tell a lie. I did cut it with my hatchet'. 'Run to my arms, you dearest boy, glad I am, George, that you killed my tree, for you have paid me for it a thousand fold. Such an act of heroism in my son is worth more than a thousand trees, though blossomed with silver and their fruits of purest gold!'

It seems that the Rev Weems was motivated both by a wish to demonstrate his hero's real character, even if fictitiously, and by an eye to sales. In the latter he succeeded, and his book went through 59 editions by 1850. It is curious that the imaginative tales it contained – the cherry tree is not the only one – should ever have been taken literally, since as early as 1810 a critic asked whether the book was to be seen as a biography or a novel.

Washington and Weems

Washington's father may well have had a cherry tree, on the 10,000 acres he owned. He died when George was eleven. But Washington (1732-1799) really needed no novel to embellish his extraordinary life, which was a crucial part of the creation of what is today the world's most powerful nation. He was certainly generally respected for his integrity, indeed idolised by many. His qualities of character, rather than military genius, enabled him to build and lead the successful Revolutionary forces. Indeed he made several blunders as a general, offset by the incompetence of those on the other side. He was chosen unanimously as the first President, and re-elected in the same way. He certainly played up to the dignity he thought fitting for this role, aided by an impressive physique (he was six feet two, unusually tall for the time, and of considerable strength) and by a partly deliberate gravitas of manner. He tried to put the Presidency above politics, and largely succeeded. Honesty was indeed one of his virtues, if of a rather more believable kind than the cherry tree story suggests. On his death, Henry Lee spoke for most Americans in calling him 'First in war, first in peace, and first in the hearts of his fellow citizens'.

Mason Locke Weems, for his part, was born in Maryland, the youngest of nineteen children, but went to England as a young man, and may have studied medicine there. At all events he was ordained a priest in the Church of England, by no less than the Archbishop of Canterbury, in 1784. Returning to America, he was a preacher for a time, but gave it up to become a traveling book salesman, and an author. He wrote biographies of several of the Revolutionary leaders, and such improving works as *The Drunkard's Looking Glass* and *Hymen's Recruiting Sergeant, or, The New Matrimonial Tattoo for Old Bachelors.* Another, *The Immortal Mentor, or, Man's Unerring Guide to a Healthy, Wealthy and Happy Life*, sounds as though it might be useful today. None, however, was as successful as the life of Washington.

Mason Weems's old home, in Dumfries, Virginia, is now a museum. And at the Plaza Bed and Breakfast, 21 Weems Street, Colonial Beach, one can sleep in the Mason Locke Weems room for $95 a night (2003), which includes full breakfast and high afternoon tea (to the English, simply 'tea').

19

GOUT AFFLICTS THOSE WEALTHY ENOUGH TO OVER-INDULGE IN FOOD AND DRINK, ESPECIALLY PORT
and it is really a bit of a joke, like piles and boils.

Sufferers will attest that none of these is any sort of joke. One can see some sort of reason for the last two causing ribaldry. Piles (haemorrhoids) by their nature, and boils often, occur in or around the buttocks and anus, which are of course simultaneously hilarious and unmentionable, at least in England. Hence that curious locution 'the back passage' (is the mouth the front passage?). Piles are swollen veins, boils are infected sebaceous glands or hair follicles. Both can be very painful, and require serious treatment.

Nature of gout
Gout conjures up a picture of an elderly gent with a foot, encased in massive bandages, propped up on a stool. An internet cartoon shows just such a character, holding a glass and proclaiming 'I laid my foot down in 1926'. Not a very good joke, and seemingly not a

very new one, as he was presumably at least adult at that time, more likely middle-aged, which would make him a hundred or more today. Gout tends to strike men between thirty and fifty (and women, more rarely, between fifty and seventy). Quite why gout should be thought funny is unclear.

'Gout' comes from Latin *gutta*, a drop, perhaps because the effect of it is like a drop of something hot or burning. It is a form of arthritis, that is an affliction of the joints, with a specific nature and usually a particular location, the big toe. It is caused by a failure of the body to excrete uric acid, which results from the breakdown of substances called purines, which occur naturally in the body, and also in various foods, meat especially offal and some fish such as anchovies, mackerel and herrings. The acid forms crystals, which when they accumulate cause acute pain, rather like severe toothache, as well as inflammation and redness. An initial attack usually lasts for a week or more and then recedes. It may never recur, but usually does so, and if left untreated with increasing severity. Eventually permanent damage may result. The condition is at present incurable, but fortunately can usually be controlled, normally by medication. There is also a condition known as 'pseudo-gout', which likewise involves crystals in the joints, this time usually the larger ones, the guilty substance being calcium pyrophosphate dehydrate.

Gout is among the oldest known human afflictions, and its supposed association with rich living led to it being once known as 'the disease of kings'. Michael Flanders and Donald Swann reinforced the idea with the line '...port is a drink I can well do without – it's simply a case of *chacun a son gout*' (so have some Madeira, m'dear!). And indeed excessive alcohol is among the risk factors for gout, though it seems plebeian beer is worse than plutocratic port. Alcoholic beverages don't contain much purine, but when alcohol is metabolised it raises the level of uric acid in the blood. Foods containing high levels of purines are obviously also factors, as is an erratic pattern of eating. Other factors include medical conditions such as high blood pressure, diabetes, narrowing of the arteries and saturated fats in the blood. There is also a genetic component in the causality. And as mentioned there are differences between men and women.

Port wine

Gouty men appear in eighteenth century caricatures. It may be that gout became more frequent at a time when the country was becoming ever more prosperous, and more people were able to afford a meat rich diet (the roast beef of old England). They could also afford the relatively new port wine. Wine has been imported into Britain from Portugal for hundreds of years, in particular from Porto (Oporto) on the River Douro. It is said that some English Crusaders, stopping off on the way to the Holy Land, found that Ferdinand I of Castile was busy fighting the local Saracens, and thought they might as well do their Crusading nearer to home. They liked the local wine, and took some back to England. But it was not port, simply a standard red wine.

Port was developed in the early eighteenth century, perhaps initially from the practice of adding various things to poorish wine to give strength and flavour. By mid century Dr Johnson was able to formulate his recipe, *'No, sir! Claret is the drink for boys, port for men. But he who aspires to be a hero, must drink brandy!'* Brandy or grape spirit is added to make a fortified wine (others are sherry, Marsala, Malaga, Madeira and some lesser known varieties). This also enables it to travel better, and to improve with keeping. Fine port improves in the bottle – 'laid down'. If the cartoon character had laid down port, rather than his foot, in 1926, however, he would, apparently, have done better to wait for 1927, a vintage year. Nothing to do with gout really, but it's nice to know these things.

20

HOT CROSS BUNS ARE HOT. ONLY THEY AREN'T, ARE THEY?

And then there is that pub where they hang up a new bun every Easter. What's that all about?

Well, maybe few people think that the buns with a pastry cross on top actually are hot. The name seems to have lost all meaning, and one sees them labelled 'hot-cross buns', as though it were the cross that is hot. They are sold cold, of course. Perhaps there is a vague notion that they are 'hot' because they are spiced, though the taste is never particularly hot. They retain some connection with Easter, though supermarkets sell them all the year round. As late as 1976, however, Christina Hole, in *British Folk Customs*, claimed that eating them at breakfast on Good Friday morning 'is a custom which still flourishes in most English households'. I rather doubt it. On the other hand a friend tells me that as a boy some forty-five years ago he was sent out to buy the buns, hot as they should be, that is, freshly baked.

The tradition

Traditionally, they were supplied by bakers, and hawked around by street vendors with the cry '*One a penny, two a penny, hot cross buns / If you have no daughters, give them to your sons / One a penny, two a penny, hot cross buns.*' Alternatively they might be made at home, early on Good Friday morning. Part of the tradition was that they must be made on the day itself. Another part was that they were the only thing that could be eaten on that day, a fast day. Dr Johnson in the mid eighteenth century records eating 'a cross bun' before going to church, 'to prevent faintness'.

There is no exact record of when they came to be incorporated into the Easter rituals. There is apparently a case of something like them being distributed to the poor at St Alban's Abbey, by a Father Thomas Rocliffe, in 1361. But their origins are very much earlier, and they are almost certainly pre-Christian. Two petrified loaves with crosses were preserved at Herculaneum when Vesuvius erupted in 79 CE. They *might* have been Christian at that date, but some other ritual purpose seems more likely. Small cakes, made of wheaten flour and marked with a cross, were eaten by Greeks and Romans at the Spring equinox, well before Christian times. It has been alleged, perhaps fancifully, that the cross was originally a Tau (like a T with a loop on the top), the Sign of Life and of Tammuz, the ancient Middle Eastern god of fertility and vegetation. Tammuz died, went down to the nether regions, was resurrected and returned to earth, and finally ascended to heaven.

Survival

Certainly Easter is a time of rebirth in nature, and, consequently no doubt, in various religions. Easter buns or cakes had magical significance. They were thought to protect against harm, and it was believed that they would never go mouldy – which in fact, if properly made and kept, they seldom would. They would just dry out. This was made use of for medicinal purposes. Buns were hardened in the oven and hung from the kitchen ceiling. When needed, they could be grated and mixed with milk or water to relieve various ailments. In some places the remedy was given to cattle also. They would be replaced every Easter. The custom apparently persisted in some places into the twentieth century.

But with the advent of Protestantism the preservation of buns was seen as superstitious, and Queen Elizabeth I is said to have commanded that they be confined to their proper season.

At The Widow's Son pub, in Bow, East London, a hot cross bun is hung up each Easter. The story is told, and repeated every year in the media, of a widow whose son, at some uncertain date, went to sea but never returned. Each year she set aside an Easter bun for him, and this has been zealously perpetuated in the pub which replaced the poor old lady's cottage. It's all Lombard Street to a China orange, as they used to say, that this is one of the numerous examples of a story that has been made up to explain a ritual, the original meaning of which has been forgotten. Of course there may have been a widow and a lost son, such combinations must have been frequent in former times. But hanging up an Easter bun was even more common.

21

THE IRISH POTATO FAMINE WAS DELIBERATELY CAUSED BY THE BRITISH GOVERNMENT
so as to starve and subjugate the Irish people.

This, or something like it, is certainly thought by some, if not by anyone of moderate education. In 1996, the State of New York passed a law requiring the story of the famine to be taught in all public, i.e. state, schools. The Governor, George Pataki, in signing it, stated: 'History teaches us that the Great Irish Hunger was not the result of a massive failure of the Irish potato crop, but rather was the result of a deliberate campaign by the British to deny the Irish people the food they needed to survive.'

No reputable historian would accept this for a moment, and the actual school curriculum presents a more balanced version. But some of the forty million Americans who regard themselves as 'predominantly Irish' probably hold Governor Pataki's view. They may in turn have contributed towards the funds of the IRA in the mistaken belief that they were helping to right an ancient wrong, when they were actually perpetuating conflict and bloodshed.

The Irish famine

In fact, the events were quite frightful enough without distorting history. Famines have occurred frequently throughout human history and still do so in many parts of the world, with great loss of life and immense suffering. They happened in the history of both Ireland and Britain, and 'the' potato famine was one of several. It stands out partly because of its severity, and partly because of its place in the often sorry story of relations between the two countries. This was made explicit at the time, for example the Rt Rev John Hughes DD, Bishop of New York, in a sermon at the Broadway Tabernacle on 20th March 1847, traced the story of conflict back to the Norman invasion of Ireland in the twelfth century.

Without making light of it, one might say that the famine was a tragedy waiting to happen. The immediate cause was an attack of the potato blight *phytophthera infestans*, an airborne pathogen probably originating in North America, in 1845. This blight affects both growing and harvested potatoes, rendering them inedible. In this year it destroyed perhaps 40% of the Irish crop, and next year virtually all of it. Further attacks followed for three or four years. Such attacks had occurred before, and did later. But this time it was particularly disastrous, for several reasons. Working backwards from the event, as it were, the first of these was that the range of potatoes grown in Ireland had become largely restricted to one variety, the *lumper*. Then, the diet of very many, perhaps 90%, of the Irish population had in turn become largely restricted to potatoes. They were cheap and easy to grow, and combined with milk do provide a relatively nutritious diet. These were recent developments. In the eighteenth century oats, barley, rye, beans and green vegetables had been widely grown.

In the eighteenth and nineteenth centuries there was a large increase in the Irish population, exacerbated by the return of soldiers after the Napoleonic Wars ended in 1815. Most Irish farmers were tenants of mainly Protestant landlords, who controlled some 95% of the land, and under the system of inheritance, their holdings tended to become smaller as they were divided between heirs, until they were only just able to support a family, and then only by depending on the productive potato. Furthermore, in 1801 the Act of Union removed the semi-independent Irish Parliament, in favour of control from Westminster. Many landlords moved from Ireland to England, leaving their estates to be run by agents, whose interest was simply to extract the landlord's rents, and maximise his profits by continuing to export most crops (and other products such as butter) other than the potato.

The consequences

The net result was a famine which led to the population dropping from about eight to less than six million, from death and from emigration. Tragically, too, the famine occurred when the political doctrine of *laissez faire* was dominant. It was genuinely thought by many of those in authority that interference in what was believed to be the natural course of events would not only not improve things in the long run, but actually make them worse. Despite this, Robert Peel, then Prime Minister, did authorise, without waiting for Parliamentary approval, the import of quantities of corn (maize) from America. The prevailing theory of trade was that it prospered best when duties were low or non-existent. There was an exception to this as a policy, namely protection for the farming interest by taxes on the import of grain – the Corn Laws. The Irish famine added to a powerful campaign to get rid of these, which was done in 1846. The government did make various attempts to alleviate conditions, but not very effectively. Some, such as the institution of workhouses, were themselves a source of hardship. A good many private initiatives, especially by Quakers, sought to relieve the suffering. Even some landlords joined in. But in general it was all far too little.

The full story has been told in, for example, *The Great Hunger: Ireland 1845-1849* by Cecil Woodham-Smith (1962), and *Ireland Before and After the Famine* by Cormac O'Grada (1993). The Irish famine was not the result of a malign policy, but the outcome of numerous factors, only a few of which could have been understood, foreseen, or prevented. Had the blight struck with such virulence a few decades earlier or later, the effects would have been far less serious. As it was, there was intense human suffering, and there were far-reaching political and social consequences for Ireland and the rest of the British Isles, and indeed the world, through the emigration of so many justifiably embittered, but also energetic and talented, Irish people to the USA and elsewhere.

Today we might consider that far worse famines, at least in terms of numbers, are occurring in many parts of the world, while richer nations seem little more able to relieve them than in the 1840s. And farming policies, particularly in the European Union, are deliberately restricting the variety of crops that may be legally grown. The possible implications are clear, or should be. As has been said in so many contexts, those ignorant of history are condemned to repeat it.

22

JESUS WORE A BEARD
and had long hair, as seen in innumerable pictures of him.

Certainly Jesus is commonly represented, in art and in films, as having a beard and fairly long hair. To some religious groups it is a matter of importance, one way or the other. A Tabernacle Baptist group, for example, feels that hair and beard are typical of rebellious youth, and quite unfitting for their Saviour (though some other Christians feel that Jesus *was* rebellious). They take their stand on First Corinthians 11:14, 'Doth not nature itself teach you, that if a man have long hair, it is a shame unto him?' But this does not help with the beard. And on the other hand there is Leviticus 19:27, 'You must not cut your side locks short around, and you must not destroy the extremity of your beard'. Jesus as a good Jew would surely obey.

The image of Jesus
Of course there are no authentic contemporary portraits of Jesus. There have been numerous depictions purporting to be such, usually of miraculous origin. The most famous today is no doubt the Shroud of Turin, allegedly the sheet in which Jesus's body was wrapped after the Crucifixion, and on which a representation was miraculously imprinted. The Shroud is a typical mediaeval

production, as is conclusively shown by carbon dating and by analysis of the actual image. It dates almost certainly from about 1270 to 1350. When first reported it was condemned as a fake by the religious authorities. It still has many adherents, as mere facts do not deter the faithful. There are and have been numerous similar images, such as the Mandelion of Edessa, supposedly a towel on which Jesus wiped his face, leaving his portrait behind. Just why these things should happen is unclear, it seems a clumsy way for God to perpetuate an image, if that is what he wanted.

There are quite a lot of fairly early, though not contemporary, descriptions of what Jesus looked like. Some of them form part of the writings which were ultimately rejected as authentic parts of the Bible, the *Apocrypha*. Others come from various Church fathers. Unfortunately they do not agree. Some say he was very beautiful, others not. Some give him a black beard, or a brown one, or none at all. (Of course there is no reason why he should not have had a beard sometimes but not always.) The earliest graphic art again sometimes shows a beard and sometimes not. Sometimes his face is shown as black (leading some modern black people to claim him as one of themselves). But it must be remembered that religious art, from the earliest times and still today, is often not intended to be taken literally. Mediaeval paintings of, for example, saints voyaging across the sea, show the saints as far larger than the boat they are in. They are much more important, and the boat is simply a message to indicate their mode of travel.

Similarly the early depictions of Christ give an ideal representation, not an attempted portrait. The beardless ones seem to be conveying the idea of a perfect, undying youth, whereas a beard indicates strength and manliness. In classical Greek art, a beard indicates an adult, its absence a youth. It seems that early on, the first form was associated with the living Jesus, and the latter with the ascended Christ. The artists making such images were of course supplying the needs of their customers, and doubtless painted according to demand. And as E.H. Gombrich showed clearly (in *Art and Illusion*, 1977), artists copy other artists. Religious art has always been produced by workshops, in which apprentices are trained to produce what sells. Only the greatest of them make major innovations.

Sources of Christianity

Christianity, like probably every other religion, took over much of its imagery, and indeed its doctrine and mythology, from what was already there. The early images of Christ are often very similar to those of Apollo. A statue of Apollo carrying a sheep or lamb on his shoulders, from sixth century BCE Athens, is almost identical to one of Christ the Good Shepherd from fourth century CE Rome. From the figure of Serapis there is Christ as king and judge, from those of Greek sages wisdom and compassion, from Antinous the perfect youth, from Dionysus grapes and wine, from Alexander and from Roman emperors the image of a conqueror. All were pressed into service by the new religion.

In just the same way the events of the life of Christ are paralleled elsewhere. The divine conception, the baby who is recognised as marvellous but must be hidden from danger, the precocious youth, the temptation, the preaching, the miracles, the betrayal, condemnation and sacrificial death, followed by resurrection and ultimate return – all are elements in many other faiths and mythologies, often extant in the early years of Christianity. This, plus the virtually complete absence of any evidence for Jesus's life outside the Bible itself, has led many to doubt that he ever existed at all, let alone with a beard or long hair. My personal guess, and it is no more, is that there probably was an itinerant charismatic preacher some two thousand years ago, around whom all these legends accumulated. It does seem often to be the case that apparently fictitious traditional stories turn out to have some root in real events, like the grain of sand in the pearl – the Trojan Wars, or King Arthur, for example. Then again, many of the recorded sayings of Jesus have an air of the sort of fragments that might well survive in oral tradition – soundbites, in modern terms. But we shall probably never be certain. And for the beard, we shall have to fall back on Saint Augustine, who stated clearly, 'What his appearance was we know not.'

In June 2005 Rosalie Lawson of Florida found the face of Jesus on a burnt potato crisp. 'It sure looks like the image of Christ to me,' she said. How the lady knows what Jesus looked like when St Augustine did not, is not explained.

THERE ARE REALLY ONLY THREE JOKES IN THE WORLD

but what they are, and how this is known, is never explained.

Well, to be honest, this is not something that everyone knows. But it does crop up every now and then, and not just in pub conversations, with an implication that it is common knowledge. Despite a lengthy search I have not discovered any source of the idea.

Theories of humour
Perhaps the closest is the various attempts to find a general theory of humour. It is generally agreed that these fall into three, sometimes four, categories. One sees all humour as involving a sense of superiority, one specifies incongruity, and one relief. A possible fourth is ambivalence. It is easy to think of cases of all four. There are two main problems, however. The first is that it is equally easy to find cases that don't conform to whichever recipe one favours. The second is that it is also easy to find cases of superiority, incongruity, relief or ambivalence that are not in the least funny.

This point was behind Ken Dodd's famous remark about Freud. Sigmund Freud's theory was a version of the relief formula. Laughter results when some repressed tendency is allowed expression. Ken Dodd, one of the greatest of modern comics, is also a thinker about comedy. As he put it, 'The trouble with Freud was, he never played first house at the Glasgow Empire on a Saturday night, when Rangers and Celtic had both lost'. (The remark has been reported with various wordings. For anyone from outer space, or the USA, Rangers and Celtic are the rival Glasgow football teams.) There is obviously far more to comedy than content. A catchphrase of Frank Carson, another fine comic though not, for my money, in the Dodd league, is 'It's the way I tell 'em!' And yet another, Jimmy James, perhaps now forgotten, used to say, 'A comedian isn't someone who says funny things. He's a person who says things funnily.' This is partly why the comedy of Shakespeare, for example, survives less well in print than his tragedy. The script needs a skilled actor to bring it to life. And as David Garrick, who was famed equally for both, remarked, 'Any fool can play tragedy. But comedy, Sir, is a damned serious business'.

The business involves among other things context, timing and audience expectation. Victoria Wood said that she found she could sometimes get a laugh by something which merely sounded as if it were going to be a joke. Tommy Cooper, another in the premier league, got one by, on a completely dark stage, giving exaggerated sighs – 'Aah-aah! (pause) AAH-AAH!' One more example from this irresistible genius. At a Variety Club lunch he was called on to speak. He stood up and looked around with his air of puzzled expectancy. The audience started laughing. At exactly the right second he bent down to his wife and said, 'I haven't said anything yet!' The audience erupted.

Old jokes, new jokes
The trouble with the original remark is that it is strictly meaningless. There must be literally millions of jokes. More are constantly being made, spontaneously and by script writers. To reduce them to three, or any small number, means squashing them so hard, so to say, that all the humour is squeezed out. It is precisely the variations that make them funny. It is much the same problem as trying to reduce people to a few types – what makes them people is individuality. This is not to say that people cannot

be measured along a few important dimensions (physically, height, weight, girth, for example). And maybe this will be possible with humour. But no one has done it yet.

What is true is that while new jokes are always being made, some jokes are older than one might think. Here are three. The first appeared as 'a new joke' in a Sunday paper in the 1990s. A boy tells his older brother that he has had sex with a married woman. Should he tell their father? The brother says yes. So he does, and the father asks who it was, but the boy will not say. The father says, 'Was it Mrs Jenkins in our street?' 'No, it wasn't her'. 'Well, was it Mrs Howard round the corner?' 'No'. 'Was it your mother's friend Mrs Smith?' 'No.' 'Well, I respect your confidence, I think you know you've done wrong, we'll say no more about it'. His brother says, 'Was he angry?' 'No,' says the boy, 'but he gave me three very good suggestions'. This 'new' joke was told by the 'Cheeky Chappie' Max Miller, 'the pure gold of the music hall', who died in 1947.

The other two have been told on television. 'Isn't it lucky,' says the comic, 'that a cat has two holes in its fur, just where its eyes come!' This found a place in Freud's book *Wit and Its Relation to the Unconscious*, 1905. Presumably it was not new then. In the other, Paddy is a sailor, and the ship is getting ready to sail. The captain says to Paddy, 'Go down into the hold, and bring us all up a pint of beer'. 'I will not', says Paddy, 'sure while I'm down there you'll sail without me!' This gem appeared in *Mrs Pilkington's Jests: Or the Cabinet of Wit and Humour*, 1759. And again it was very likely not original then.

Rather similarly, many comic *characters* are very old. The servant who is cleverer than his master (Jeeves and Wooster), the country bumpkin who outsmarts the city slickers (Crocodile Dundee), the pompous minor official (Captain Mainwaring in *Dad's Army*), the cowardly braggart (Dr Smith in *Lost in Space*), the irascible old man (Victor Meldrew in *One Foot in the Grave*) – to give just one example of each – can be found throughout classic comedy, going back to Roman times. But only three jokes? Thank heavens, no!

24

KILTS AND TARTANS ARE WORN BY ALL SCOTSMEN (AND BY NO-ONE ELSE) AND HAVE BEEN SINCE TIME IMMEMORIAL

and Englishmen wear bowler hats and carry rolled umbrellas (an item for non-British readers, if any)

The attempts we humans have made to clothe ourselves fall roughly into two styles, the cloak and the suit. Either we drape an otherwise shapeless length of material around the body, or we try to tailor something to fit, more or less. Both are found all over the world. Frocks and skirts are a sort of half-way house. Men often wear the latter, in such forms as the sarong and the kilt. Greek soldiers have a ceremonial kilt, and there are Irish kilts – it isn't unique to Scotland. But it is a source of pride to Scots and their numerous descendants in foreign lands.

How old is the kilt?
So much so that it is often thought to be very old in origin, mediaeval or even older. The historically absurd film *Braveheart* (1995) had its thirteenth century characters in primitive kilts – actually of late seventeenth century pattern. It also had them painted

blue with second century woad. The Scottish kilt derived from a garment of the cloak type, the plaid (it has various names in Gaelic). Confusingly, the word 'plaid' is now used in the USA to mean a design of a tartan type. As described by H.F. McClintock in *Old Irish and Highland Dress* (1943), the original plaid was a length of heavy material some four to five yards long and fifty inches wide. It was worn draped around the whole body (and also served as bedding when necessary, as the ancient Greeks used their cloaks). Probably during the seventeenth century the custom arose of folding it in pleats, and securing these with a belt around the waist. The next step, probably in the next century, was to divide the garment into two. It was useful to discard the upper half when heavy work had to be done. And finally someone thought of sewing the pleats to retain them permanently. There is an authentic sewn kilt, the earliest known, dated to 1792, in the Tartans Museum in Franklin, NC.

Scottish customs

So far so good. In the same century, specifically in 1715 and 1745, there were attempts, supported by many Scots particularly from the Highlands, to overthrow the Hanoverian monarchy in Britain and restore the (originally Scottish) Stuart dynasty. After the second of these was crushed, stringent laws suppressed the wearing of Highland dress. These laws also meant the end of the old traditional clan system, although they were repealed some thirty years later. At this time the Romantic movement was getting underway, with a wave of nostalgia for a past that was largely one of the imagination. 'Gothic' architecture became fashionable. Heraldry was revived. Macpherson published his poems supposedly by an ancient Gaelic poet, Ossian, and Walter Scott his historical novels. Kilts and tartans were enthusiastically renewed. A little later Queen Victoria herself adored everything Scottish, from porridge to Balmoral to John Brown her forthright servant. She had bagpipes played every morning and expected Highland noblemen to appear in appropriate dress.

Tartan is much older than kilts. Probably since the invention of weaving several thousand years ago, interlocking stripes have been used to make patterns. They were characteristic of Highland dress by the sixteenth century. But the patterns were those of individual weavers, and not particularly associated with clans. With the introduction of mechanical looms standard designs became possible, and these too fitted in with the Romantic revival. Gradually they became associated with particular names, and with the notion of clans. Today there are some 3,000 recognised tartans, some up to 200 years old, others brand new. Tartans, and even kilts, are worn by many outside Scotland with tenuous, or no, Scottish connection. 'Legitimate' versions are worn on formal occasions and by some Scottish regiments, and by some men more casually. In a way it is artificial, but at least the Scots, or those relatively few who go in for it, have managed to create a national identity in dress which is known the world over.

The English
Which is more than one can say for the English. The classic Englishman with bowler hat and rolled umbrella is rarely encountered. Bowlers are mainly seen in marches of the Orange Order in Northern Ireland, and on some ceremonial occasions. Umbrellas, of course, whether neatly rolled or not, are a frequent necessity in Britain. (A mediaeval joke has the Devil rejecting Englishmen for the fires of hell, as being too wet to burn.) The image remains, probably largely due to John Steed, played by Patrick MacNee, in the 1960s TV series *The Avengers*. The bowler itself has a specific origin. It was designed by the hatters James and George Lock, a seventeenth century firm which still exists in St James's Street, in 1850, for a customer, one William Coke. It was made for them by the firm of Thomas and William Bowler in Southwark, hence the name. (The name Bowler, in turn, meant originally a maker of bowls.) Lock's, however, still call it a Coke hat. Americans call it a derby, as they have since at least 1870, though no one seems to know why.

And I suppose we can't avoid the question. What do they wear under the kilt? There are pictures on the web showing either nothing or various garments. The answer seems to be that traditionally it should be nothing, or no more than a long shirt. But for activities like Highland dancing, briefs. And for the non-traditional, anything you like, provided it doesn't show. Though it is said George IV favoured pink tights.

25

NATIVE LONDONERS ARE KNOWN AS COCKNEYS

They talk in rhyming slang, wear clothes covered with pearl buttons, go to pubs or music halls every night, and eat jellied eels or fish and chips.

Well, maybe not everyone believes all this, especially not Londoners. But each item does crop up often enough to indicate it is believed by some people. In an episode of the television series *Murder, She Wrote* – time, late twentieth century – the heroine, Jessica Fletcher, played by Angela Lansbury, has a twin sister who is a star at a music hall on Ludgate Hill, yards from St Paul's Cathedral. No such place ever existed, and music halls had virtually disappeared by the first World War. Miss Lansbury appears ageless, but Jessica Fletcher doesn't go that far back. Music halls began as extensions of pubs, with landlords adding a room with a platform, later a stage, so that patrons while drinking could watch, and join in with, mainly singing turns. They developed into, or were superseded by, variety theatres akin to American vaudeville. Both were killed off by the cinema (Bob Hope added that 'when vaudeville died, television was the box they put it in').

Pubs

Pubs (public houses) have survived better, and in the last few decades some have repeated the pattern, offering live music, mainly rock and pop, occasionally jazz, comedians, strippers etc. Others have turned into 'gastropubs' offering more or less pricey food, or into cocktail or tapas bars, or still worse 'theme' pubs such as the wholly bogus 'ould Oirish' places. Some remain as friendly and well stocked drinking places, sometimes with good basic food. But overall they are in decline, closing, in London, at two or more a week. Mostly they are converted into far more profitable flats. Londoners use pubs less and less. The English have a genius for creating something remarkable, and then abandoning or destroying it. Dr Johnson held that 'there is nothing which has yet been contrived by man, by which so much happiness is produced as by a good tavern or inn'. Charles Dickens would have agreed, and there are still a few where both would have felt at home. Catch them while you can.

Traditions

'Pearlies', dressed in black suits or dresses decked out with patterns of 'pearl' buttons, the ladies with ostrich feather hats, can be seen on occasion, usually in connection with a charitable event. Nowadays they are all Pearly King or Queen of some district in London, as is stated (in buttons) on the back of each costume. Their children are Pearly Princes and Princesses. I heard a visitor enquire how you got to be a Pearly King or Queen, to be told 'Oh, it's handed down, dear, from generation to generation!' This is true, but it is relatively recent, at least in the scale of London history. Pearly decoration seems to have begun in the latter half of the nineteenth century. The first 'King' is said to have been Henry Croft (1862-1930), a poor boy who wanted to collect money for charity, and developed a more elaborate costume in 1875. Four hundred Pearlies are said to have attended his funeral. There are fewer now.

Fish and chips can still be found readily, even in central London. Jellied eels are also still on sale though much more rarely, sometimes in the few remaining original nineteenth century shops, along with meat pies, mash and liquor (mashed potato and parsley sauce). All are losing out to take-away Indian, Chinese, pizza and the ubiquitous burger.

Rhyming slang is more complex. Allegedly it was originally a thieves' slang designed to baffle the authorities. It involves, of course, substituting for one word another, or a phrase, that rhymes; and then, often, leaving out the bit that rhymes. So 'head' becomes 'loaf of bread', and then 'loaf'. 'Use your loaf' is probably still in use, and would certainly be understood by anyone. So would 'Rosy (Lee)', 'tea' and 'butcher's (hook)', 'look', and 'cobbler's (awls)', 'balls' in the sense of 'rubbish' - not the male appendages. Here the second element is never used, and is probably generally forgotten. On the other hand 'tea leaf' for 'thief' is never, I think, shortened.

There are no established rules, and there is no fixed vocabulary, although there are numerous purported 'dictionaries' in print. Rather, it is a manner of speaking, used by a few older people unselfconsciously, and by younger ones deliberately for effect. The effect is usually either a sort of light-hearted, joking attitude, or a dumbing down, part of the 'mockney' affected by some better educated persons, presumably to show they are really of the people. Rhymes come and go. Thus for example 'arse' has long been translated into 'Khyber (Pass)'. But it might now also be 'Haagen (-Dasz)'. In a further extension, it can be 'aris': 'Aris (totle)' – 'bottle (and glass)'. Of course there's far more to London speech than rhyming slang, see *Cockney Past and Present* by William Matthews, 1972.

Cockneys

'Cockney' probably comes from Middle English *coken-ey*, a cock's egg, that is a small, misshapen one, used for a townsman, later localised to a Londoner. A tradition developed that true Cockneys were born 'within the sound of Bow bells', that is those of St Mary-le-Bow church in Cheapside, once a market in the heart of the City of London. 'Cheap' is from Anglo-Saxon *'ceap'*, a market, a bargain being referred to as 'good cheap', that is inexpensive. Now hardly anyone lives within sound of the bells, and in quite recent times the maternity ward at the ancient nearby St Bartholomew's Hospital was closed. Thus there are, strictly, few if any new Cockneys. But words live and evolve regardless of facts, and some Londoners will still think of themselves, or be considered by others, under the old name.

26

LORDS OF THE MANOR IN MEDIAEVAL TIMES ENJOYED THE *DROIT DU SEIGNEUR* WITH EVERY NEW BRIDE

and when they went away they kept their own ladies secure with chastity belts, some of which can still be seen.

The famous *droit du seigneur or de cuissage*, in Latin *ius primae noctis* or right of the first night, of course meant the local lord taking each new bride that he fancied into his bed, before, presumably, returning her next day to the impatient bridegroom. It really does appear to be a complete fantasy. There is no hard evidence that it ever actually happened. That does not completely prove that there never was such a case, but it was clearly not a generally recognised custom, as has often been supposed. On the other hand the idea has been around for a very long time. It occurs in the first recorded epic of Western literature, the story of Gilgamesh, around 1900 BCE. It is found in stories of classical Greece and in Semitic and Celtic cultures. And from the fourteenth century it becomes popular in mediaeval European tales.

A persistent fantasy

It is still going strong. It featured in the film *War Lord* (1965) with Charlton Heston. and in *Braveheart* (2002), the wife of the Scottish hero, William Wallace, is a victim of it. However, this does not accord even with the traditional fiction, let alone with historical reality. In the traditional version, only serfs, just a cut above slaves, were subject to this particular duty. Wallace is in the film, and was in reality, a nobleman, the feudal vassal of an overlord.

Various reasons have been proposed as to why the fantasy was so popular in the late Middle Ages, and has persisted. Obviously it does make for some dramatic stories, with elements that have always served story tellers well – romance, sex, power, aristocracy and so on. And as indicated, the story has run and run. It is suggested that the theme of lordly power was particularly intriguing at a time when the old feudal system was breaking down. Lords were striving to retain their position, and serfs or ex-serfs were resenting it. See *The Lord's First Night* by A. Boureau and L.G. Cochrane, 1998.

Possible origins

Then again, there have certainly been real traditions in some societies which in some ways are a parallel. Ritual defloration of a bride, by someone other than the husband, is recorded in Eurasia and in the Pacific. Generally, this is associated with the idea that first intercourse, and in particular blood, are dangerous or unclean. This is much different to the European fantasy, but, like the ancient literature, it does show that the basic idea has been widespread. And it did percolate into the West in the supposed travels of Sir John Mandeville. These told of a voyage from St Albans to China and back between 1322 and 1356, and of the many wonders to be found in distant lands. The book was written in French, and turned into Latin before English and several other languages.

No one has ever been able to establish whether Mandeveille made all or any of the voyages he recounts, or indeed who he actually was. Many of the marvels were widely current, often clearly based on travellers' tales, such as great castles on the backs of elephants (obviously howdahs). Mandeville tells of an island 'where the custom is such, that the first night that they be married, they make another man to lie by their wives for to have their maidenhead; and therefore they take great hire and great thank … For they of the country hold it so great a thing and so perilous for to have the maidenhead of a woman, that them seemeth that they that have first the maidenhead putteth him in adventure [risk] of his life'.

Chastity belts

Chastity belts have the curious feature that they are more real now than they were historically. In February 2004 ABC News reported that alarms were set off at Athens airport by what turned out to be the metal chastity belt worn by a woman traveller. And the internet offers many ingenious varieties, for both sexes, whose motivation may be left to the imagination. Like the *droit*, they have a long pedigree in literature, apparently beginning in the twelfth century poems of Guigemar de Marie de France, where they appear as a symbol of chastity by a boy and a girl. An illustration of one appears in a book on military equipment written in 1405, and they are mentioned by the Abbé de Brantome (1540-1614) in his racy *Lives of Gallant Ladies*.

It seems likely that if they were actually used at all, probably in the sixteenth and seventeenth centuries, it was for only short periods, and then voluntarily by women as a form of protection. Without going into the distressing details, it is obviously very difficult to design anything that would serve its ostensible purpose over a long period without extreme personal discomfort.

The myth perhaps developed in Victorian times, and it is then or later that the supposed mediaeval examples in museums were produced, either as novelties or as outright fakes. There were, however, those who recommended this sort of thing as a way to prevent masturbation. The horror of this natural occurrence began in the early eighteenth century and reached its height towards the end of the nineteenth. The wheel has turned, if not full circle, certainly 180 degrees, as masturbation is now recommended as healthy and desirable.

Chastity belts today are either a minor kink, or a joke, as in the anonymous mock folk song popular some years ago, in which a young gallant and his lord's wife are thwarted by the master having 'fitted a Yale, nonnie nonnie', while away on the Crusades, until a page boy steps forward to 'open it up with my duplicate key, nonnie nonnie'.

27

A MAN AND WOMAN WHO LIVE TOGETHER FOR SOME TIME ARE DEEMED TO HAVE CONTRACTED A 'COMMON LAW MARRIAGE'

and marriage has always been between one man and one woman, for the purpose of raising a family, and authorised by religious or other authority.

A recent poll (mentioned in an article in *Family History Monthly*, March 2004, on which I have drawn below), found that half of those responding believed that a man and a woman living together resulted in the status of 'common law marriage', conferring legal rights on the participants. At least in England and Wales, this is not so, and has not been for two and a half centuries. 'Common law' refers to the body of principles and rules regulating ownership and disposal of property, and the behaviour of individuals, which have the force of law from long use and general acceptance. In contrast there is statute law formulated and enacted by government. The latter may amend or cancel what has been accepted even for hundreds of years, and this is what happened with marriage.

Legal marriage

Up until the eighteenth century, marriage could be contracted in various ways, at least in England. The simplest was just a promise between a couple to take each other as partners. That itself might be taken as binding, or it might become so on consummation. One reason for this relatively informal approach was to limit the number of illegitimate unions and children. The view seems to have been that partnerships and offspring would occur anyway, so it was better to accept things and bring them within legal society. Many mediaeval arrangements were similarly unsystematic but practical.

The more modern view is that everything has to be systematised, and anomalies ironed out. In our own day this has reached epidemic proportions. The Marriage Act of 1753, often called the Hardwicke Act after the Lord Chancellor who introduced it, laid down that a marriage would only be valid if conducted by a priest, before at least two witnesses, in the local parish church. It had to be preceded either by obtaining a licence, or by publishing banns in relevant parish churches on the three Sundays beforehand. Exceptions were made for Quakers and Jews but for no-one else. In addition, parental consent was required for those under 21. However the minimum age for marriage was 14 for boys and 12 for girls (raised to 16 for both in 1929). Non-Anglican churches, and registry offices, were approved for the ceremony in 1836. In America, English common law was adopted by the original thirteen states and by all subsequent ones except for Louisiana, which inherited Roman law from France. About a dozen have some form of common law marriage.

Forms of marriage

These changes illustrate in a small way that marriage has taken many different forms throughout history and in various cultures. The philosopher A.C. Grayling has pointed out that 'marriage' in fact refers to two different things. One is a description of fact, that two (or sometimes more) people are living together in a sexual relationship on a more or less permanent basis. The other is the social regulations and customs, often given the force of law, that may seek to control such relationships. Although Grayling does not say so, these in turn are of two kinds, civil and religious (at least in the West). Sometimes only one is operative, or only one is necessary, sometimes both. In our society, legal marriage carries not only individual rights and obligations but many other implications, as for example for taxation and inheritance.

The usual norm is, of course, one man and one woman. But many variations have been accepted at various times. Polygamy, one man and multiple wives, is not so uncommon. The Mormon Church practiced it for fifty years, only abandoning it in 1890 – and some individual Mormon families still continue on this basis. The reverse, several husbands per woman, is much more rare but has existed. So have same-sex marriages, about which there is currently such a fuss. Of course these have always occurred, probably in every society, in the first of Grayling's senses. Couples have simply lived together, openly or covertly. At times when this was socially disapproved, such as the nineteenth century, a thin veil was sometimes drawn, such as 'friendship', or one partner might adopt the other as a son or daughter.

John Boswell, in his scholarly work *The Marriage of Likeness* (1994), has argued convincingly, if controversially to some, that in Europe from classical times and into the Middle Ages, same-sex unions were not uncommon. Indeed with the growth of Christianity, they were often marked by church ceremonies and priestly blessing. This was true in both the Roman Catholic Church, whose doctrine was and is that the couple marry each other (Do you take this man...?) The priest sanctifies the event. In the Orthodox Church, in contrast, the priest marries the pair.

Rules and rights
Although the heterosexual family couple is the obvious norm, in most societies marriage has fulfilled many other functions, often to do with finance, property, or dynastic liaisons. It has been governed by all sorts of rules, about for example marrying within or outside various groups, such as religion, race, class, caste, or clan, and forbidding or allowing various degrees of relationship, such as brothers and sisters, or the wives and husbands of these. For example, some societies have made it the norm for a bereaved husband to marry his wife's sister, while others have forbidden it.

The current Western model, in which a man and a woman simply choose to marry, or now very often to live together, mainly from mutual affection, is historically relatively rare. And there really seems no reason why any such couple, of whatever sex, should not enjoy, if they wish, the legal status of marriage as well as the actuality of it. This should not be affected by any rules that a particular religious group wishes to live by. It has no right to impose them on others.

28

MATHEMATICS TRAINS THE MIND
or it may be Latin and Greek, or history, or whichever subject one is defending.

Usually, the claim is made about a subject that does not appear to have any immediate practical use. (A legendary academic remark is, 'Here's to pure mathematics, and may it never be of the slightest use to anyone'.) One does not often hear accountants or engineers justifying their courses on such grounds. Their claim is to train accountants or engineers. And they are right. Mathematics does indeed train the mind – to do mathematics. And it is also the case that mathematics is very useful in many fields, so it also could be said to train for these, to a greater or less extent depending on how much maths is involved.

'Mental muscles'

But the claim is, usually, that the chosen subject does more than this. It teaches the student how to think, reason, memorise, solve problems etc. Or, going even further, it strengthens the 'mental muscles', in the sort of way that push-ups strengthen arms. A headmaster under whom I suffered for some years taught Latin, claiming specifically that what we were doing was like a boxer training with a garden roller (I wondered whether they really did). 'He doesn't take it into the ring with him!' he would say. And very often the claim is that a particular subject has a special virtue – Latin, or maths, or whatever, is the best of all subjects.

The physical analogy is false. The mind is not like a muscle. Indeed the mind is not physical, though it is inseparable from a physical structure, the brain. The mind/brain does benefit, particularly in the course of development, from both physical and intellectual input. A healthy diet, and a stimulating environment, are both necessary. From the educational point of view, this means a range of intellectually interesting and demanding subjects, including, but by no means limited to, the conventional school curriculum. It may be the case that some of these are more beneficial in general than others, but no one has so far demonstrated this. On the other hand it certainly has been shown that a very restricted input harms development. The extreme cases are those unfortunate children who are every now and then discovered, who have spent most of their childhood alone or sometimes with animals. They are always handicapped and in severe cases never recover. Milder cases are those whose educational diet consists entirely of learning by heart some religious text, an intellectual impoverishment as unjustified as depriving a child of essential vitamins or proteins.

The question of what psychologists call transfer of training has been investigated experimentally for over a century, and despite the experiments becoming more thorough and sophisticated, the early findings still broadly stand. If you want to learn something, it is best to tackle it directly. It is less successful to learn or practice something else, and hope that it will somehow rub off. The best way to master a tennis serve is by serving, of course with instruction, monitoring and feedback. That's why all top players have full time coaches.

Learning to think

It is just the same with mental skills, but it is seldom done so systematically. University teachers consistently claim that their aim is to improve 'critical thinking', or an equivalent phrase. What they turn out to mean is 'effective thinking'. But when asked how they do this, they can seldom really answer – often falling back on the idea we started with, that 'critical thinking' will result from whatever they are teaching. And indeed, if they are good teachers, to some extent it will. A student who learns to assess historical, or scientific, or literary, evidence and reach a conclusion can, to some extent, transfer this to other situations. But there are two caveats. One is that each subject has its own style of argument. Other situations may yield other sorts of evidence and require other sorts of reasoning. Second, the student needs tutoring in this very business of transferring his skills; or rather, in seeing what is general in the skills and how they can be applied. This is usually left to chance.

'Critical thinking' can be taught. There is much research showing how to do it. One excellent analysis is given by Professor Diane Halpern of California State University (in the journal *American Psychologist*, 1998). She distinguishes four elements, all of which need to be specifically developed. One is a readiness to do the hard work that thinking requires (as all skills do). A second is the skills themselves – such things as understanding how cause is determined, recognising and criticising assumptions (not taking things for granted), analysing means-goal relationships, giving reasons to support conclusions, and so on. Third is training in analysing problems to see their structure, and thus how thinking skills can be applied to them. And fourth is standing back to check for effectiveness and monitor progress toward a goal. Most high level subjects incorporate some of these to some extent, but not systematically. (There are also numerous pop psychology books claiming to teach one to think, usually with little sound foundation but based on gimmicks.)

The idea that certain subjects 'train the mind' almost certainly goes back to mediaeval higher education. A student's early years were spent on skills that would be generally useful. 'Grammar' (as in grammar schools) was Latin, which was necessary for the study of any subject, and indeed for any sort of professional career. 'Dialectic' was logic and reasoning; 'rhetoric' was persuasive communication. These and other skills prepared the student for training in any profession. Some notion of this persisted into modern times, at least at Oxford and Cambridge, so that graduates in classics were thought best suited to run a vast Empire. But in most universities education has become more and more specialised, and we have in a sense come full circle by once again asking what sort of general education we should provide, as well as what specific subjects. 'Critical thinking' or 'training the mind' might well be part of it.

29

MEDIAEVAL WARFARE CONSISTED OF HORDES OF HEAVILY ARMOURED KNIGHTS ON HORSEBACK CHARGING AT EACH OTHER

wielding lances, swords, battle-axes, maces, morning stars* etc.

Well, in the first place it depends on what you mean by 'mediaeval'. The ending is relatively simple, although all historical periods are arbitrary, and things hardly ever change absolutely overnight. But such events as Columbus's first voyage (1492), printing with moveable type (mid fifteenth century), the Reformation (Luther's 95 theses, 1517), the Tudor monarchy (1485), mark a significant shift around 1500. When the Middle Ages began is more debatable. Some historians take the period to

---

* (A morning star was an iron ball studded with spikes, attached to a chain which in turn was attached to a short staff.)

begin with the Norman Conquest, 1066. Others put it right back to the collapse of the Roman Empire. But this itself was not one single event – Edward Gibbon took six large volumes to tell the story, and the Eastern empire hung on to an increasingly precarious, but continuous, existence until the fall of Constantinople in 1453.

A thousand years of knights?

The great historian of mediaeval warfare, Sir Charles Oman, took as his starting point the Battle of Adrianople in 378. Rome had already split into East and West, and the Eastern Emperor Valens faced a force of Visigoths and Ostrogoths under their leader Fritigern. Valens had sent for reinforcements to the Emperor of the West, who was his uncle Gratian. For reasons over which historians have argued ever since, he attacked without waiting for help to arrive. His Roman infantry, which had been supreme in warfare for centuries, were overwhelmed by Goth horsemen. Oman claimed that this was the start of 'the thousand year reign of the knight'. He wrote it first in a student prize essay in 1884, and repeated it in successive editions of his book *The History of War in the Middle Ages*, for the next forty years. His thousand years ended with the Battle of Crécy in 1346, when English (in fact, largely Welsh) archers destroyed a much larger French force with mounted knights to the fore.

More recent historians explain that the whole thing was, as usual, far more complicated. The Goth cavalry were nothing like knights as later ages knew them. Technically, the crucial step for the armoured knight was the introduction of stirrups, which came surprisingly late. They seem to have been invented in China around 500, but took two or three hundred years to be generally adopted in the West. Without them, heavy armour and weaponry on horseback are impossible. Even more fundamentally, the mediaeval knight was the outcome of many later developments, economic, social and military. And, as always in history, they had numerous different manifestations, and they did not stand still but constantly changed and developed.

The image most people have is, no doubt, that of innumerable films and other media. A warrior encased in plate armour, so heavy that he has to be lifted on to his horse, which is similarly armoured. He has been made a knight after a complicated ritual, ending with being touched on the shoulder by the sword of his sovereign, to whom he owes complete loyalty. Or alternatively it may be done spontaneously after some act of bravery.

Knights in legend and reality

There is some truth in all this. Armour did eventually become so heavy that it restricted the wearer's mobility, especially if dismounted, but only by about the fourteenth century. The complete suit of plate armour was later still. Knighthood did develop elaborate rituals, and codes of behaviour, though there were many variations. Some knights without patrimony were effectively mercenaries. Rules of honour were far from universally followed. At some periods, it was knights themselves who initiated others into the order. (See *The Knight and Chivalry*, 1974, by Richard Barber.)

There is also some truth in the comparison often made with the modern tank. The heavily armed knight was faster than infantry, and could traverse more difficult terrain. In the right circumstances he could be unstoppable. But knights were vulnerable. Mounted, they could be disabled by good archers, or their horses could be shot from under them (something avoided in film portrayals). The crossbow, slow to load but powerful, could pierce plate armour, while the longbowman could get off five or six shots a minute with a penetration not far short of a rifle bullet. Dismounted, a knife or sword could get into joints in armour. And the knight hardly advanced at all in weaponry. Archery and early firearms were too cumbersome for use on horseback, and in any case were the weapons of peasants. Knights were also, like tanks, extremely expensive, compared to infantry. Mediaeval armies might consist of one of the first to five or more of the latter.

Much of mediaeval warfare involved sieges, and in these the knight only came into play in storming a breach, which by no means always happened. Much, too, was as Bismarck later put it, diplomacy carried on by other means – demonstrations of strength rather than outright battles, which were both risky and costly. And knights could be an unreliable weapon. Codes of honour, and the quest for individual glory, often led them to hopeless acts of valour for their own sake, rather than wise tactics. On the other hand, warfare could, for the noble participants, be largely a commercial venture, with rich rewards in sacking a city, or in ransoming prisoners. These too might make knights less useful to a general. The knight of romance was a part of mediaeval war, but only one. His role was exaggerated from the first, by contemporary chroniclers and song-makers, and has been ever since, while the image has become stabilised at a point that was, in fact, very nearly the end of a long process of change.

30

'MOTHERING SUNDAY' IS MOTHERS' DAY
Well, you could say it is now. But it wasn't always so...

Some weeks before Easter, shops and television urge us to remember 'Mothering Sunday – Mothers' Day', and buy presents, or at least cards, for our own mothers. It has become in many ways, like other regular festivals, a commercial occasion, which is not to say that many people do not celebrate it with genuine affection.

In praise of mother
Celebrating motherhood has very ancient origins. In one way or another it appears in many religions. In the West, the Greeks held the spring festival of Rhea, wife of Cronus and mother of the gods

and goddesses of Olympia. In Rome, Cybele was the mother goddess, whose festival of Hilaria, a joyful occasion whose name gives us 'hilarity', occurred on 15th to 18th March. In the old legal calendar based on terms, and at Oxford University, the Spring term was called the Hilary term.

Mothering Sunday developed in the Middle Ages as a church festival, on the fourth Sunday in Lent, when the faithful would visit their 'mother' church, that is the church in which they had been baptised, or the Cathedral of their diocese, taking gifts with them. In the seventeenth century the practice grew up of young men and women who were away from home, perhaps as apprentices, returning home with gifts for their mother, at the festival. They were often given a holiday for the purpose. The gift sometimes took the form of flowers, or of a 'mothering cake'.

The cake was a 'simnel' cake, and Mothering Sunday was sometimes called Simnel Sunday. According to Christina Hole's book *British Folk Customs* (1976), simnel cakes were, and are, of three types. The Shrewsbury cake is rich and dark, covered with a thick almond paste (marzipan or *marchpane*), and decorated with candied fruits. The Devizes cake is star-shaped, without the almond paste; and at Bury it is flattish, usually round and full of currants. The name probably derives from simila, the Latin word for the fine wheaten flour that was used. As very often happens, stories have arisen to account for the word, no doubt when its original meaning was forgotten, involving either a man named Simon, or Lambert Simnel, the imposter to the throne in Henry VII's reign. However, simnels were mentioned in the *Annals of the Church of Winchester* as far back as 1042.

Inventing Mother's Day

Mother's Day, properly so called, is an American invention, due to Anna M. Jarvis (1864-1948) of Philadelphia. Her mother, to whom she was greatly attached, died in May 1905. Miss Jarvis thought that an annual event would be a good way to celebrate, not just her own, but all mothers. The idea caught on and the first official Mother's Day was on 10th May, 1908. By 1911 every state in the USA had adopted it, and in 1914 Congress made the second Sunday in May a national event. It has since spread to perhaps most countries of the world, though not necessarily on the same date. In Norway for example it is in February and in Argentina in October.

In Britain it retains its Lenten date, but the two events have merged to become one. No doubt this has been partly under the specific influence of American service people during the two wars, and to commercial interests in getting customers to buy presents. A gift for Mother is much more profitable than a visit to a church. In March 2006 a reader protested to *The Times* about all this. *The Times* responded, no doubt rightly, that it was 'a rising tide of modern usage which we may well be unable to turn back'.

It might be seen as yet another example of American 'cultural imperialism', the (largely unintentional) dominance of the mores of the most powerful nation. Thus, Guy Fawkes Day and Bonfire Night have virtually disappeared in last few decades, to be replaced by Hallowe'en. Of course that is an ancient European custom, but it is the American version that has come back to us, with its carved pumpkins and 'trick or treat'. (Bonfires, much older than either, still persist.) Father Christmas is now Santa Claus, again a European creation who has returned in, literally, American dress – the short red coat and floppy hat. Fish and chips, pie and mash, fall before the universal burger, and so on.

Father's Day was apparently conceived by Sonora Smart Dodd in 1909 on the model of Mother's Day, and declared to be the third Sunday in June by President Calvin Coolidge in 1924.

31

NERO FIDDLED WHILE ROME BURNED

Well, not actually fiddled, perhaps, but what did he do? And did he really throw Christians to the lions?

The Emperor Nero, Lucius Domitius Ahenobarbus, was born in 37 CE, and reigned from 54 to his suicide in 68. He has generally had a very bad press, being seen as one of the maddest and most tyrannical of the rulers of Rome. The two features that most people know are as above. The actual saying that he 'fiddled while Rome burned' has been around at least since 1649, though its origin is obscure. It can't be literally true because bowed instruments, from which the fiddle and related instruments developed, did not appear in Western music before the ninth century. But the allegation that Nero sang and played the lyre while Rome was in flames goes back to his own day.

Nero the Emperor

The constitution of republican Rome began to disintegrate about 90 BCE, in a series of power struggles which eventually ended with the victory of Octavian in 31. As the Emperor Augustus he began a system of government, the Principate, in which power was concentrated in one man, and passed on by various combinations of inheritance, adoption, assassination, bribery and warfare. Erratic as it seems, the system maintained the Empire in some form, and often with great success, until its final extinction with the fall of Constantinople in 1453. Such a system depends on the nature of the individual holding power. Nero came to office through a series of intrigues and deaths, some of them certainly murders. He may or may not have been directly involved in the death, which may or may not have been murder, of his immediate predecessor Claudius.

Nero had some of the qualities of an effective ruler, and a good many deficiencies. At least in the earlier part of his reign, the Empire was well administered, often through former slaves who had shown ability, and were often educated Greeks or Orientals. The population of Rome itself was kept happy by the now traditional methods of free food and entertainment ('bread and circuses'). Nero was no soldier and was averse to war – both a strength and a weakness. Personally he could be violent and ruthless, especially if he felt threatened. This led him to kill his own mother, the equally unscrupulous Agrippina. His sex life was certainly depraved and bizarre. What was particularly unusual, however, was that he was far less interested in administration, or even power, than in success as a connoisseur of the arts, and as an artist himself, a poet, singer and actor, as well as an athlete and charioteer.

On the night of 18th July 64, there broke out what proved to be the most destructive fire ever experienced by Rome. Nero was at Antium, on the coast some distance from Rome. He returned at once and organised relief and measures to limit the fire. After raging for six days it was eventually put out, only to break out again on a smaller scale. Somehow, however, the rumour took hold that Nero himself had started the fire, perhaps to clear ground for a new palace which he did in fact later build, the

113

Golden House, some of the remains of which can still be seen. It was widely believed, also, that, inspired by the spectacular sight, Nero sang an epic of his own composition called *The Fall of Troy*, accompanying himself on the lyre. This may or may not have been true, but it was the start of the 'fiddling' legend.

Persecuted Christians

The resulting extreme unpopularity caused Nero, or his advisers, to seek a scapegoat for the disaster. They picked on the sect of Christian believers. These people were already generally unpopular, and relatively defenceless. There were many exotic religions in Rome, looked on by traditionalists as dangerous superstitions. Christians were seen as especially odd, as a particularly bizarre Jewish sect. They shared with other Jews an objection to accepting the Emperor as supreme ruler. The Romans, like the Greeks, considered the Jewish practice of circumcision to be barbarous and unnatural, as indeed it is. The Jews as a whole were a less suitable target, however, because of political sensitivity in the Middle East.

Christians, too, were even more isolationist than Jews. Their talk of universal love suggested to outsiders orgies of promiscuity and incest. The symbolism of the Eucharist, the body and blood of Christ, suggested cannibalism. Above all, Christians then still believed in the imminence of the Second Coming of the Messiah, accompanied by destruction of the world in flames. This not only threatened the existence of both everyday life and of the Roman state, but made it seem plausible that Christians had actually tried to set the process in motion.

At all events, it seems that numbers of Christians were slaughtered, often with bizarre cruelty: torn to pieces by wild animals, crucified, or made into blazing torches after dark. Such extreme persecution in fact turned even the hardened population of Rome even more against the Emperor. The Christians themselves, of course, survived and eventually became stronger. They had always had a tradition of martyrdom, stemming from Christ himself. And in Christian legend, these new martyrs became further proof of the power of faith. Christian writers almost certainly exaggerated the persecution, and their version eventually became official. As to Nero, in parts of the Empire where his policies had been beneficial, he continued to be admired after his death. Legends arose that he was not dead but would return. But in the Christian tradition he developed into the Great Beast 666 in the *Book of Revelation of St John the Divine*, written towards the end of the first century. And further, into the Anti-Christ, the evil counterpart of Christ who like him would return in the last days.

Two more balanced accounts are *Nero* by Michael Grant (1970), and *Nero: The Man Behind the Myth* by Richard Holland (2000).

32

NOSTRADAMUS FORETOLD THE FUTURE
including the French Revolution, Napoleon, the rise of Hitler, the assassination of John F. Kennedy and his brother, and so on and so on...

Nostradamus was Michel de Nostredame (1503-1566). Born at St Remy in Provence, he became a physician and apparently had some success with unorthodox methods. Details of his life are sparse, but he seems to have travelled a good deal before settling in Marseille and then in Salon, where he died. His house is now a museum. He was an astrologer and mystic, interested in prediction and prophecy. From 1550 onwards he published an annual almanac of predictions, and from 1555 produced prophecies in verse form, nearly all in four lines. These were eventually published as a whole in 1568. They consist of 942 quatrains, four line verses, arranged in sets of one hundred, known as centuries (and one set of 42). They are in (mediaeval) French, with some words from other languages including Latin and Greek.

Interpretations
Pretty well from their appearance, the quatrains have been interpreted and argued over, the issue being what, if anything,

they predict. The literature is now vast. The British Library public catalogue, not all its holdings, lists 225 items, nearly all, to judge from the titles, attempts to find meaning in the verses. Although interest in them has never ceased, it took a surge forward in modern times thanks to the writing of Erika Cheetham (1939-1998). According to her own account, when studying mediaeval French at Oxford, she one day asked for a book in a library, but by mistake got a copy of Nostradamus's quatrains. Intrigued, she eventually published three books of interpretations. Nostradamus has become an industry, complete with gift shop, society of followers, an International Centre and some 350,000 websites. Even the most academic of bookshops normally carry half a dozen items This has all had an extra impetus from the 500th anniversary of Nostradamus's birth in 2003.

The quatrains are in no particular order and are unconnected to each other. They are also in extremely obscure language, and there is no indication of how this is to be understood. There are virtually no specific names or dates, and even when there are, the reference is far from clear. Furthermore, there is disagreement over the meaning of some of the old French words, or in some cases even over what Nostradamus actually wrote. Thus, interpreters are pretty free to apply each quatrain as they will. The plan has generally been to choose some dramatic event that has already happened, and try to find a quatrain that can be made to fit, when translated.

Thus, after the attack on the World Trade Centre and the Pentagon on 11th September 2001, the following was quoted:

L'an mil neuf cens nonante neuf sept mois / Du ciel viendra grand Roy deffrayeur / Resusciter le grand Roy d'Augoumois / Avant après Mars reguer par bonheur.

(Translation: The year 1999 seven months / From the sky will come the great King of terror / To resuscitate the great King of the Mongols / Before after Mars reigns by good fortune.)

Making meaning

'From the sky' is true enough, but only extreme ingenuity can make any of the rest apply to 7/11. Such ingenuity is not lacking, but it is entirely unconvincing to anyone who is not a dedicated Nostradamist. It is exactly the same with all the other quatrains and their supposed referents. The faithful explain the difficulty first, by saying, correctly, that Nostradamus himself stated that he disguised his meaning. However, that does not help us to know what it was. Second, it is suggested that he might have had only partial glimpses of the future, as it were through a mist. And thirdly, he might not have understood what he saw, for example such things as airplanes or the effects of atomic bombs. These arguments explain why, for example, when he foresaw the rise of Hitler, he wrote 'Hister', or 'Ister' in some versions. Either he did not get the name exactly, or he used the name of a region near the Danube to mean Hitler, because the latter was born not far away. Why he should disguise a name that would mean nothing for nearly five centuries is not clear.

Of course, in such ways one can make anything mean virtually anything else. In a delightful twist, immediately after 7/11 another quatrain appeared on the internet which, with the usual obscurity of course, predicted the event. It turned out to be a hoax, some lines written long before by a student to illustrate just the ease of wild interpretations. Even an attributed date a hundred years after Nostradamus did not, seemingly, give the game away.

It is significant that the interpretations always follow the event they are supposed to have predicted. In other words, they do not actually predict anything. But perhaps the whole thing falls most conclusively on the fact that there is, as far as I am aware, no reason at all to doubt the commonsense view that no one can see the future, for the very simple reason that it does not exist. Events have no existence until they occur, and the future may be quite different even from what seems likely. There is a crucial difference between prediction and prophecy. Weather forecasts predict what is likely to occur, given the present situation and our knowledge of meteorology. Prophecy tells what will happen. It is a form of magical thinking, and there are no grounds for believing in it.

There is available a website (getodd.com) which offers a brand new quatrain in response to any question you care to pose, created by a computer programme. The result is just as useful, or not, as any of those of the sixteenth century seer.

33

OSTRICHES BURY THEIR HEADS IN THE SAND

in order not to be seen. And elephants never forget, and swans can break a man's leg with a blow of their wing, and lemmings regularly commit suicide.

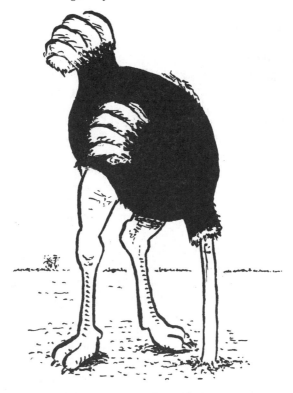

The image of the ostrich sticking its head in the sand, in the absurd belief that if it cannot see, it will itself be invisible, is such an effective metaphor for a foolishly or wilfully ignorant person, that it has become a cliché. President Woodrow Wilson remarked in 1916 that America must not be an ostrich, with its head in the sand, but he was certainly not the first. It is unclear how the idea arose. One suggestion is that ostriches were seen scooping out the hollow in the sand that serves as a nest. Another is that they sit on this nest, and in order to be inconspicuous lie as flat as possible, with their long neck stretched along the ground. It does not help, but we can recall the words of Ogden Nash:

The Ostrich roams the great Sahara.
Its mouth is wide, its neck is narra.
It has such long and lofty legs,
I'm glad it sits to lay its eggs. (1957)

Animal memories

The proverbial remarkable memories of elephants are another mystery. The classical Greeks had a saying that the camel never forgets, which is just as strange, especially since camels are not native to Greece. Nor are elephants, of course. 'Saki' (H.H. Munro) in 1910 added that women and elephants never forget an injury, but again it was already familiar. Elephants do have unusually large brains, the largest of any land mammal, of the order of one eight hundredth part of total body weight. But it is the ratio that is important, and this compares with one fiftieth part for humans. However, a recent report (2005) says that elephants react differently to elephant bones and tusks, compared to those of other species. This might suggest 'remembering'.

There is a popular myth that 'we never really forget anything'. The magic word 'really' makes the statement impossible to test, since any apparent forgetting is covered by it. Conversely any unexpected recovery of a memory is taken as evidence for the idea. It is possible that the notion can be traced to a misunderstanding of Sigmund Freud's theories. He believed he had shown that some 'forgotten' memories could be recovered. But neither he nor any serious scientist has ever asserted, as far as I know, that everything is remembered – by humans or any other species.

The elephant, or camel, idea possibly arose from some anecdotal accounts of individual animals surprisingly seeming to remember something. A study of elephant herds in Kenya in 2001, by Karen McComb of the University of Sussex, found that they formed small groups of several females and offspring, dominated by an older female. The older females were better at recognising the smells and calls of the herd. It seems that elephant memory, while not infallible, can improve with age.

Elephants, lemmings and swans

Another elephant metaphor is that of the 'white elephant', for something useless and a bit of a burden. White, that is albino, elephants do exist, and were formerly held to be sacred in Siam (now Thailand). They had to be maintained at considerable expense. Apparently they were sometimes presented by the king to someone whom he wished to ruin.

Lemmings are popularly known for rushing over the edge of a cliff, thereby committing suicide. It is hardly conceivable that any non-human creature would deliberately kill itself. The drive to self-preservation is extremely strong, and in any case suicide implies a conscious decision. What is true of lemmings, as of other species, is that they sometimes breed too successfully for their territory, which becomes over-populated. They may then attempt to migrate, and some may die in doing so, for example by drowning in trying to cross a stream. The suicide idea was perpetuated, if not invented, in a Disney animal documentary, *White Wilderness*, in 1958. This was made in Alberta, Canada, to which lemmings are not native. A small number of lemmings were imported, and filmed in such a way as to appear to be throwing themselves to their deaths.

Swans are often said to be able to break a man's leg with a blow of their wing, though under what circumstances this could occur is unclear. Authorities merely state that they can give 'a nasty blow', or the like. An ancient belief is that swans, normally mute, sing just before dying – their 'swan song', a phrase which seems to date from the 1830s. This notion is mentioned by Plato, and in English literature by Chaucer, but its origins, and the reason for it, are unknown.

As far as I am aware, zebras really cannot change their stripes, nor leopards their spots.

34

PIRATES BURIED THEIR TREASURE
Preferably on a desert island, its whereabouts shown on a map subsequently lost or stolen until eventually obtained by Our Hero who after many adventures, etc, etc...

The archetypal account is Robert Louis Stevenson's classic *Treasure Island* (1883). He created a story out of myths, legends, folklore and above all his own imagination, which has ruled the popular mind ever since. So much so that, while piracy is today a very real danger on the seas, it is often not taken seriously - by the authorities at least, though certainly by the victims. Pirates are slightly comic characters in outlandish dress, armed with cutlasses. Actually, today they use Kalashnikovs and rocket-propelled grenades. In 2004 thirty crew members were killed in attacks around the world.

All the old romance
Probably the most memorable, and caricatured, pirate of films and television is Robert Newton as Stevenson's Long John Silver, complete with crutch and parrot on shoulder crying 'Pieces of eight! Pieces of eight!'. More recently, Johnny Depp gave us an outrageously camp creation in *Pirates of the Caribbean: The Curse of the Black Pearl* (2003), and sequel.

Stevenson promises us a tale:

...of schooners, islands and maroons
And Buccaneers, and buried gold,
And all the old romance, re-told
Exactly in the ancient way...

But it never was like that. *Treasure Island* is one of the finest works of a master story teller, but realism was not Stevenson's strong suit. He was quite happy to have nutmeg trees in the Caribbean, when they belong to the East Indies. And have you ever tried to keep apples in a barrel? They'd be rotten in a week.

But to our treasure. Jim Hawkins tells us at the beginning that part of the treasure is 'not yet lifted'. Why ever not? What would be the sense of leaving it? It is almost as if Stevenson cannot bear to give up his buried treasure, even to bring it home. Admittedly it was large, £700,000 worth, apparently largely in gold. But why did the rascally Captain Flint put it there in the first place?

The fact is that pirates never did bury treasure, except in stories. Why should they? In the first place, valuables of any sort were for spending. Mostly, no doubt – and as contemporary accounts tell – they went pretty quickly, as sailors' wages have so often gone, on drink and women. 'And when our money it is all gone, we'll boldlie go to sea', as many a song had it. In the second place, booty was very often not of the sort that could be neatly buried in a stout chest, to be left indefinitely, like gold and jewels. Much was perishable and bulky – tobacco or rum, cloth or spices. And in a third and important place, the proceeds of a piratical voyage would usually be shared out among the ship's company as soon as possible. Any one share of booty would be comparatively small. Even the captain often took only two shares to the one of each of the crew. Pirates in their heyday were a surprisingly democratic bunch. Often the captain was chosen by the crew themselves, for the duration of the trip. Any attempt to carry off a substantial amount for later burial would have been looked at, shall we say, askance. And if a captain, or any other pirate, did manage to accumulate substantial wealth over time, he was much more likely to invest it in a respectable business or property, as some certainly did.

Historical pirates

Piracy has flourished, no doubt, since the first ships sailed. The story book age of piracy, however, is the sixteenth and seventeenth centuries. And the story book location is the *Spanish Main*, which properly refers to the then Spanish possessions in the Americas, but sometimes was used for just the northern coast of South America or for the Caribbean Sea. Piracy here was fostered by the desire of Spanish governments to get hold of the vast sources of gold from their new possessions. Spanish treasure ships were prime targets. Furthermore it was the habit of many governments, including the British, to grant licenses to individual vessels to plunder the merchant ships of countries considered as enemies.

The distinction between these more or less official pirates and those who went 'on the account' quite independently was often blurred. Captain William Kidd (1645-1701), one of the most famous names of piracy, but in fact a quite unsuccessful one, held royal authority to capture pirates and keep the booty. In the event he did commit acts of real piracy himself, although his subsequent trial was clearly unfair, apparently for political reasons. He actually took relatively little booty (and that was mostly cloth), but after he was hanged, at Wapping on the River Thames, legends arose of vast wealth that he must have concealed somewhere, since it was never found, and this seems to be one of the main sources of 'buried treasure'. Numerous attempts have been made to find Kidd's treasure. As recently as 1983 two men were arrested for trespassing while searching for it in the South China Sea – which Kidd never entered.

Treasures, hidden or hard to find, have been the stuff of story-telling at least since Jason and the Argonauts sought the Golden Fleece, whatever that was. But pirates in the golden age of piracy didn't, as far as we know, bury theirs on desert islands or anywhere else.

And just to add to the misery, there is very little evidence that they flew the 'Jolly Roger', the skull and crossbones – though black flags are reported. Nor, it seems, did they make victims walk the plank to a watery grave. But those are other stories.

35

PRACTICE MAKES PERFECT
**and accordingly anyone can do anything, if they work hard
enough. Or, back to Samuel Smiles.**

Samuel Smiles (1812-1904) was a politician and administrator
who had an immense success with his book *Self Help* (1882). The
lesson of the book was '...that nothing creditable can be
accomplished without application and diligence'. This fitted
excellently with 'Victorian values', and there is much truth in it.
More recently it has been revived in a new form. An article in *The
Times* in January 2004, by Dr Nick Baylis, asserted: 'Any
individual of average learning ability is capable of acquiring an
expertise in any given field ... The acquisition of lofty skills relies
not on special genes, but rather on self-motivation, a rich learning
environment and our being able to give sufficient practice time to
the subject'.

Practice is necessary
Notice first a shift from the Smiles doctrine: he asserts that
application is essential; Dr Baylis implies, if he does not quite

state, that it is enough. Second, although the implication is clear, it is hedged a little. What is 'an expertise'? Will a very small degree of skill count? And what is 'average learning ability'? Abilities of all kinds are 'normally distributed', like height. Average height can be defined as the mid point, say five foot nine, or any preferred range, say from five feet something to six feet something.

Thus, it may be true that anyone of 'average' learning ability can acquire the rudiments of chess, or tennis, or music. It does not follow that they can be a grandmaster, win at Wimbledon, or compose an opera. One really doubts whether Dr Baylis seriously believes that he could do any of these if only he had practiced enough. His argument is based on research by Professor Michael Howe, who died (sadly early) in 2002. He showed that it takes about 3,000 hours of practice to become a good amateur musician, and about 10,000 to be a concert soloist. This is in line with a great deal of other research on expertise in various fields, from sport to science. But Mike Howe (whom, if I may add a personal note, I knew well and liked), made in my view the elementary mistake of confusing a necessary with a sufficient condition. The vast body of evidence, from both research and common experience, shows that practice alone, even in favourable conditions as mentioned by Nick Baylis, is not enough.

Early learning

Preparatory schools, in the UK, are private establishments generally very well equipped, and staffed by skilled and experienced teachers, with a favourable staff-student ratio. Their pupils come from well-off homes, and in general they work hard. These schools spend great effort and time on coaching their boys and girls to get scholarships to enter public schools at thirteen. But they succeed only seldom. Nick Baylis quotes the most famous of all child prodigies, Mozart, and argues out that he was made to practice for several hours a day by his father Leopold, a skilled music teacher. But accounts of Mozart's childhood suggest that in fact he was not *made* to practice – the difficulty was rather to get him to do other things. This is very characteristic of child prodigies. They seem spontaneously drawn to a particular field, and show talent even before they begin to practice seriously – in music by singing, or picking out tunes on the piano, for example.

Srinavasa Ramanujan (1887-1920), born into a poor family in India, with little schooling or access to books, became virtually untaught an exceptional mathematician, the implications of whose ideas are still being studied. Certainly he worked at it, but why? Bertrand Russell (1872-1970) was introduced to Euclid at the age of eleven. 'This was one of the great events of my life, as dazzling as first love. I had not imagined there was anything so delicious in the world.' Not many of us would say this.

Developing potential

The other side of the equation is that there is ample evidence that human potential, of all kinds, physical and mental, has a strong genetic component. The evidence comes first from behavioural genetic studies, e.g. of twins, and now from unravelling the genetic code itself. How important the genetic component is varies from one area to another. And it does not necessarily mean that genius runs in families, in fact this is rare. Rather, each individual gets a selection of genetic elements, and the genius gets, as it were, a winning hand. And it always requires an appropriate environment, and practice, or equivalent, for full development. The Bach family produced about seventy members who went into the music business. But only one, Johann Sebastian, is acclaimed as a supreme genius. It is not plausible to attribute this to hard work alone, even in a good learning environment.

This in no way suggests that children should not have opportunities to develop whatever potentials they have. Some may have a wider range of, or more flexible, possibilities than others. Certainly motivation (itself partly genetically determined), opportunity, good teaching, and continued practice, are also all components of high achievement. And all must be well balanced. We might recall the Zen master whose pupil asked how long it would take him to achieve enlightenment. 'You must work five hours a day for ten years', said the Master. 'But Master, I am desperately eager for enlightenment! I will work ten hours a day! How long will it take me then?' 'Twenty years', replied the Master.

36

PROFESSORS ARE ABSENT MINDED

and probably a bit nutty. And academics called 'Doctor' are not real doctors.

Professors are not absent minded. Now just where did I put those notes? Only joking. But not only can I find no evidence that professors are particularly forgetful, I can't find anything to suggest how the idea arose. Yet it has become, not so much a belief as a cliché, a more or less automatic association. Thus Alan Greenspan, Chairman of the American Federal Reserve Board, is described as looking, despite his expensive suit, 'like a forgetful professor'. *The Absent Minded Professor*, played by Fred

MacMurray in the film of that name in 1961, forgot his own wedding in the excitement of research. And so did his successor Robin Williams when it was remade in 1997 as *Flubber*.

Students and their teachers

Further back, 'Saki' (H.H. Munro, 1870-1916) wrote of a professor who 'resembled the aristocrats after the French Revolution, except that whereas they had learned nothing and forgotten nothing, he had learned everything – and forgotten everything'. Student stereotypes no doubt have played a part. Students notice much more about their teachers than the latter, perhaps, do about them, although not always accurately. At least they usually know the name, whereas it is extremely difficult to remember the names of often several hundred students, even after meeting them individually. This may look like absent mindedness. It is also the case that, until recently and even now to some extent, academic life allowed eccentricity to flourish. Academics were often appointed quite young (as they still are, it's cheaper), and then largely left alone, particularly once they had reached the rank of professor. Today, the pressures are all towards conformity and, many would say, mediocrity. Academics have been reduced, it was said a few years ago, to 'workers in the knowledge factories'. Now, I think it is more like slaves in the graduate mines. But they are not generally absent minded.

There does not seem to be any foundation for a persistent myth about one supposed example of professorial absent mindedness. This involved students using what psychologists term 'operant conditioning'. One can train animals to do tricks or make particular responses by regular small rewards, at first for behaviour that is in the general area that is wanted, then progressively 'shaping' it more closely. Animal trainers have long done something similar, of course. The mythical students trained their professor, when lecturing, to do some odd behaviour such as scratching an ear, or repeating a particular phrase, by smiling and nodding whenever it occurred. Of course this could not have worked had the victim noticed it, so he or she must have been absent minded. Unfortunately, though, there seems to be no evidence that it has ever been achieved.

Professors are not a strictly defined class. Punch and Judy practitioners traditionally term themselves 'Professor', and there is nothing to stop them. In the USA most academic grades carry the title, differentiating it by adding Assistant, Associate, Adjunct, Full, or other terms. Holders are often referred to simply as 'Professor', rather as a Major-General is called 'General'. In European universities, at least in modern times, that is the last two centuries (modern for institutions that originated eight hundred years ago), the title 'Professor' has been accorded either to very distinguished persons or to heads of departments. For a long time these were often the same thing. Now, heads have become largely administrators, while the title is awarded much more freely, although still usually on the basis of academic merit.

Professors and Doctors

Understandably, the general public often use the term more loosely. Back in the days of radio, Dr C.E.M. Joad was a national celebrity, and frequently called Professor Joad. He was Head of the distinguished Department of Philosophy at Birkbeck College, but never, in fact, carried the title 'Professor'. Confusion is much worse when it comes to 'Doctor'. Most people understand this to mean a medical practitioner, indeed one can say that this is now the accepted meaning. The odd thing is that, at least in the United Kingdom, the large majority of medical doctors have no such term among the letters after their name. Even more oddly, many of the more highly qualified specialists and consultants do have it, but prefer not to use it, calling themselves Mr, Miss or Mrs as the case may be.

'Doctor' is a degree awarded by a university (and some other institutions), whereas Professor is a title. 'Doctor' originally means 'teacher', because one of the marks of a mediaeval university was the acceptance of its senior graduates to teach in other universities. This was the *ius ubique docendi*, the right to teach anywhere. To begin with, 'doctor' was awarded to those qualifying in one of the then three major professions, law, medicine and theology. The peculiar history of English universities (only Oxford and Cambridge until the nineteenth century) was that they largely lost their original professional functions. One result was that intending physicians came to take only a first degree of Bachelor, and this they still do. Your GP is nearly always a Bachelor of Medicine and Bachelor of Surgery (of course very few now do much of the latter, though some still see patients in a Surgery). But they are styled Doctor by long custom

Academics, on the other hand, usually do have a degree of Doctor, indicating an advanced training in their discipline, and have to suffer the minor irritation of being 'not a real doctor'. It could be tidied up if the medical profession would use 'Bachelor' for their pre-clinical training, and 'Doctor' for the professional qualification. Other countries do this, so that your American practitioner has MD, Doctor of Medicine (medicinae doctor), after his or her name. In Latin, *medicus* was the person who gave treatment, and French follows this with *médecin*. But we English love complexity, especially if historically rooted. And it wouldn't solve the academics' problem. But they have so many nowadays that they probably hardly notice this one.

37

PSYCHIATRISTS, PSYCHOLOGISTS, PSYCHOTHERAPISTS AND PSYCHOANALYSTS ARE ALL 'SHRINKS'

Or if you will, loony-doctors. And they typically work sitting behind the patient, who lies on a couch.

A news item today tells that the University of Edinburgh is offering a course in 'pet psychotherapy', or 'how to psychoanalyse your dog'. It turns out to be a short course in animal behaviour. It is not possible to psychoanalyse a dog or any other non-human. This is because the process is based on speaking.

Some definitions
But to go back a bit. These 'psych-' words are not legally defined, at least in the UK, nor are they necessarily used in quite the same way in different countries. But their usual professional uses are these, briefly.

Psychiatry is the study and treatment of mental and behavioural disorders. Psychiatrists are normally medically qualified persons who have specialised, as others do in gynaecology or paediatrics, and so on. They use various methods, some involving drugs, occasionally surgery, often group or individual behavioural therapy or counselling, etc.

Psychologists normally have a first degree in the basic science of psychology, which covers all aspects of the development of human behaviour from infancy to old age, and all the factors that affect it: genetic and environmental; physical, social and individual. Only some graduates in psychology go on to practice, for which usually a further specialist qualification is needed (often a professional doctorate). In the UK they then normally have the status of Chartered Psychologist.

'Psychotherapist' is a looser term that can be applied to anyone who treats people by mainly non-physical methods.

'Psychoanalyst' should properly be restricted to those who use the particular methods originally developed by Sigmund Freud (1856-1939). They are usually but not always medically qualified, before their specialised training. Of course some individuals may have more than one qualification, say in both medicine and psychology.

Freud and psychoanalysis

Freud is a good starting point for more detail, since it is certainly he who gave rise to the popular image of the couch and the analyst, typically with a beard, heavy glasses and a foreign accent. Freud had all these, and he did use a couch (a genuine one of his can be seen in the Freud Museum in London). Freud was trained as a (medical) doctor, and hoped for an academic and research career, but entered private practice to support his family. He became interested in disorders that seemed to have no obvious physical cause, and at first tried treating them by hypnosis, for which purpose he used the couch that he never afterwards abandoned. But early on he developed instead a method of letting the patient talk about anything that came into their head – 'free associating'. He elaborated the theory that all our behaviour, normal as well as 'abnormal', is influenced by patterns laid down early in life, particularly in relationships with one's parents. Controversially, he regarded these patterns as essentially sexual.

Furthermore, the patterns are normally 'unconscious', kept out of awareness because they are too disturbing. But they can be laid bare by the analyst, who interprets what the patient says and does, in terms of its deeper meaning.

Thus the patient can come to understand and master the reasons for his or her behaviour. Freud's ideas, at first rejected, were quite quickly widely accepted, and by his death he was one of the most famous people in the world. Undoubtedly he radically changed the way we think about ourselves, for better or worse. At the most general level, it is true that human beings are much less rational and in control of what we do, than we might like to think. But evidence in support of Freud's very elaborate theory, and the effectiveness of his treatment, is largely conspicuous by its absence. That has not stopped it being extremely influential. And some of his intuitive insights are currently being re-examined in the light of modern research.

The science of Psychology

Psychology has different roots. It began as, and still is, the attempt to apply the normal methods of science to human beings. That frequently means sophisticated experimental design and statistical analysis, since human behaviour is the result of so many variables. The approach is applied in numerous specialised areas. Clinical psychology overlaps with psychiatry in dealing with disturbed behaviour. Not many try to trace problems back to early childhood, though that can be important in some cases. Educational, occupational, forensic or criminological (not much like TV's *Cracker*), health, counselling, market research, sport. are some other applications, all dealing with the range of normal behaviour. Probably no such psychologist uses a couch. And it isn't 'all in the mind'. Sports psychologists, for example, are concerned with motivation certainly, but also with the most effective training methods, leadership, etc. The variety of methods actually used is too great even to list here (if interested, look at *Applied Psychology*, edited by R. Bayne and I. Horton, Sage 2003).

Psychiatrists are 'shrinks' if that means they deal with problems. But they do it using the methods of medicine. Psychotherapists might be so labelled, but the word covers too many varieties to generalise. All of these professions are distinct from each other. None of them shrink heads, and the expression is really simply one of abuse, or perhaps of rather anxious amusement.

38

QUEEN VICTORIA WAS NOT AMUSED
In fact, she was a dowdy old frump dressed in black, with a sour expression, dedicated to stopping anyone's fun and was, well, Victorian.

Queen Victoria reigned from 1837 to 1901, the current British record, and her best known, in fact perhaps her only widely known remark is We are not amused!

When the Queen was not amused
It seems generally agreed that she did say this once, though there is dispute as to the occasion. One suggestion is that it was after a performance of the Gilbert and Sullivan operetta *HMS Pinafore*.

But the best attested story is that it happened when a young Groom-in-Waiting (one of the varied ranks of courtiers), named the Honourable Alick Yorke, and rather a favourite of the Queen, told a joke to a German guest at dinner. Hearing laughter, Victoria demanded that the story be repeated for her benefit. Rashly, Yorke re-told an unexpurgated version of what turned out to be a bit risqué (unfortunately it's not recorded). It is not clear whether on this occasion the Queen was using the formal, royal 'we', or speaking of herself and her Ladies in Waiting who were also present.

But the remark has come to seem typical of Victoria and indeed of her era. The first is far from the case. Many first hand accounts of the young Victoria, once ascending the throne had freed her from her mother's apron strings, reveal her as vivacious and lively, with a great sense of humour, in fact both amused and amusing. Her marriage to Albert in 1840 was one of joy and happiness (though she did not care for the resultant frequent pregnancies) and they shared many amusements, from visiting the theatre or opera, often two or three times a week, to playing children's games. It was Albert's death in 1861 that put Victoria into permanent mourning, both emotionally and in the black clothing she wore thereafter.

When the Queen was amused

For some time she largely withdrew from public life – 'the Widow of Windsor'. But in later years, while she never ceased to remember Albert, the old sense of fun re-asserted itself. There are many stories of her being amused in the numerous biographies of her (for example, Christopher Hibbert's *Queen Victoria: A personal history*, 2001). Her old interest in the theatre revived, in the form of private performances at Windsor, sometimes by professional companies but often got up by members of the Court. The Queen herself closely supervised these productions, choosing the play, attending rehearsals and often adding to the script.

Visitors frequently commented on her good spirits, for example one guest, after attending a formal dinner, later told his son 'The Queen was extraordinarily vivacious, full of smiles and chaff – a most wonderful thing'. It is true that at other times she could be severe, or gloomy, especially when she had to entertain some person she disliked. One was Prime Minister William Gladstone, who she said addressed her 'like a public meeting'. But on less formal occasions there are many references to her frequent spontaneous laughter – 'the Queen laughed very much', 'the Queen laughed more than ever', 'she was immensely amused and roared with laughter, her whole face changing and lighting up in a wonderful way', 'she was very funny at the evening concert...in excellent spirits and full of jokes' (Maid of Honour Marie Mallet, quoted by Hibbert).

It is related that at luncheon on one occasion, an old and deaf Admiral was boring the Queen with an account of the recovery of a sunken ship. To change the subject she asked him how his sister was. He replied, 'Well ma'am, I am going to have her turned over, take a good look at her bottom and have it scraped'. Victoria was obliged to hide her face in her handkerchief while she shook with laughter.

The Victorian age, now beyond living memory, has come to stand for rigidity and repression, and absurd restrictions on all kinds of behaviour that are now taken for granted. Victoria and Albert certainly did preside over, and thereby foster, a marked change in social customs as compared with the more rumbustious eighteenth century and Regency periods, and an emphasis on decorum and correctness. But the age which produced Gilbert and Sullivan, a host of brilliant stage comedians like Dan Leno and George Robey, and comic writers such as Dickens, Jerome K. Jerome (*Three Men in a Boat*) and at the very end, Britain's greatest, P.G. Wodehouse, had a Queen who was most certainly, and frequently, amused.

39

RUGBY FOOTBALL WAS INVENTED WHEN WILLIAM WEBB ELLIS PICKED UP THE BALL AND RAN WITH IT

And for good measure, baseball was invented by Abner Doubleday, and cricket began in the village of Hambledon in Hampshire.

The story of Master Ellis's innovation, allegedly in 1823, is complicated. It seems to go back to 1876, when an ex-pupil of Rugby School, Martin Bloxham, who had left in 1820, wrote an account, for the school magazine, of the origins of the School's famous game, based on hearsay. It was promptly denied by a contemporary of Ellis. By this time the game was spreading far beyond Rugby itself. The Rugby Football Union was formed in 1871. In 1895 a group of old Rugbeian members of the RFU, who wanted to keep control of 'their' game, set up a committee, which promulgated the Ellis story. It was investigated by a journalist, J L Manning, who concluded it was a hoax. Webb Ellis was now dead, but several of his contemporaries agreed with Manning. Nevertheless a stone commemorating the supposed event was placed in the headmaster's garden.

Origins of football

The fact is that in William Webb Ellis's day football was far from an organised game with generally accepted rules. At Rugby, as no doubt elsewhere, boys met beforehand to agree on rules for each major game. Running with the ball, or not, was one of the many variations that occurred to fertile minds, like tackling, hacking (kicking an opponent's legs), barging, heading and so on. Eventually two main forms of football emerged in Britain, one with a round ball propelled only by feet or head, and one with an oval ball which could be handled as well. No one person invented this. Other variations still exist, for example Gaelic football in Ireland, and several forms which are confined to one school – Eton, Winchester, Harrow. There are even some forms dating back to mediaeval times in which whole villages play against each other. Rugby itself split into two versions, Union and League, while the American and Australian rules are yet further formats derived from it.

Baseball

The legend that baseball was invented by Abner Doubleday is somewhat similar. It is perhaps not now generally believed, but for a time was accepted by many. It was supposed that Doubleday, who was born in 1819, invented the whole game and drew up rules for it, in 1839, at Cooperstown, NY. This story dates from the late nineteenth century, and seems to have been based on a letter from one of his old schoolmates, but was perhaps pushed by owners of the by then professional teams, who wanted to promote baseball as a purely American game. In fact Doubleday was a cadet at West Point in 1839, and was never in Cooperstown. There is no record of his even referring to baseball, let alone claiming to have invented it, and there was no mention of it in his obituary in the *New York Times* when he died in 1893. He had been a distinguished soldier.

There are records of baseball being played well before 1839, in both America and England. It was one of a group of related games that emerged from spontaneous folk sports, the other major one of today being cricket. They are clearly related, being distinguished from most games in having two sides who take it in turns to perform quite different functions. One side bowls or pitches a ball, which the other side tries to hit, in such a way as to score. They then change over and the originally bowling side tries to exceed the score set by the other.

Cricket

The mythology of cricket has been, not that it was invented by one person, but that it first appeared in the small Hampshire village of Hambledon, centred on the Bat and Ball Inn (a version of which still exists), in the mid eighteenth century. In fact cricket and related games were endemic in the south of England from unknown times. In 1629 the curate of Ruckinge in Kent was up before the local Archdeacon's Court for having played cricket with boys and 'other very mean and base persons to the great scandal of his minsterie'. The wardrobe accounts of King Edward I for 1300 mention equipment and clothes for his son to play at 'creag' – probably though not quite certainly cricket. Some say it was created by shepherds, using their crooks as bats and a hurdle as a wicket. But shepherding is of all occupations essentially a solitary one; you would seldom get two shepherds, let alone twenty-two, together on the downs, though they might foregather in the pub.

The most likely thing is that on some unknown number of occasions some young men or boys hit on the idea of one of them chucking a ball or a stone, which another tried to hit away. Perhaps next came the idea of 'scoring' by running between two points, or alternatively in a circle marked out in some way. This line led ultimately to baseball, while another variation, the addition of a target defended by the batter, led to cricket. In some early versions of cricket, using only two stumps, there was a hole in the ground between them, into which the batsman had to put his bat to score a run. Possibly, this was once, in some variations, the whole target. The ball was, we know, bowled along the ground, and maybe stumps were added to make the target more obvious – but this is pure speculation.

From at least the seventeenth century, the village sport was taken up by some of the increasingly wealthy nobility and gentry, both to play it themselves and as an excuse for betting. By midway through the eighteenth century bets of five hundred or a thousand guineas were not uncommon – at least £100,000 now. Rich men employed good players on their estates so that they could play for the local team. The resulting mix of amateur and professional players persisted until the early 1960s.

Hambledon became legendary, first because of its players who, at their peak from around 1770 to 1800, could take on and beat 'All England' teams. Second was the involvement of the local gentry, who were mainly responsible for organising the game into a formal club, with official dress and regular social meetings, not just for playing. The Rev Charles Powlett, son of the Duke of Bolton, was the leader here. Third and most important was the literary tradition which began when John Nyren, a former player, published in 1833 his *Young Cricketer's Tutor*, to which he, or possibly a more professional writer, added reminiscences of 'the cricketers of my time', an inspired panegyric which has been unceasingly and deservedly quoted ever since.

The Rugby World Cup bears the name 'William Webb Ellis', possibly the only international trophy to be named after a fictional event.

40

THE SANDWICH WAS INVENTED BY THE EARL OF SANDWICH

whoever he was, so that he could eat while continuing to gamble.

It seems that we may owe the name of the now ubiquitous comestible to the Earl But the story has become embroidered in various ways. A correspondent in *The Times* in 2005 was quite sure it was a servant who provided the Earl with meat between two slices of bread, while another asserted it was in order to save the playing cards from getting greasy. One internet re-telling places the incident unequivocally in 'the Beef Steak Club, a restaurant'. The Beefsteak Club, which still exists, is and was a club, not a restaurant, whose members meet to eat beefsteaks. Whether they ever gambled as well I do not know. The Earl is portrayed as not only an inveterate gambler, but as an incompetent and corrupt politician and a serial womaniser.

The Earl and his sandwich

The only contemporary written account of the incident is by a foreign visitor to Britain, one P.J. Grosley, who published *A Tour to London; or New Observations on England and Its Institutions.* He wrote:

> *A minister of state passed four and twenty hours at a public gaming table, so absorpt in play that, during the whole time, he had no subsistence but a bit of beef, between two slices of toasted bread, which he eat without ever quitting the game. This new dish grew highly in vogue during my residence in London: it was called by the name of the minister who invented it.*

This was supposed to have taken place in 1756, when the Earl was a Cabinet Minister and extremely busy. He was very hard working, arriving early and continuing late. At that time dinner was the only substantial meal of the day, and was usually taken at about four o'clock in the afternoon. It is more likely that the sandwich made its appearance on the Earl's desk, rather than at the gaming table.

John Montague (1718-1792), fourth Earl of Sandwich, was, according to the only major biography of him (*The Insatiable Earl* by N.A.M. Rodger, 1993), an active and capable politician for some fifty years. He was a man of wide interests, a musician and poet, a patron of music and the theatre, and a keen sportsman – cricket, tennis, skittles, yachting and fishing. He was a linguist, a classicist and orientalist, a traveller in his youth and later a patron of explorers and an amateur of history, astronomy and numismatics.

But he does not seem to have been a heavy gambler in the style of so many eighteenth century aristocrats. For one thing his income was, for his class, relatively small – there were many peers with ten times his money. A convincing detail comes from the betting book of White's Club, the oldest gentleman's club in London, which still exists in St James's Street. Sandwich was a member for forty-four years, but his name appears in the book only three times, one bet of twenty guineas, one for an unstated sum, and one entry in a twenty guinea sweepstake. This was at a time when to win or lose £500 pounds in a night was not remarkable – at least £50,000 now. Until he was about thirty he was regarded as something of a model of rectitude, but later gained a reputation as a libertine, which it seems was not altogether unjustified, although his exploits pale before those of many of his contemporaries.

As a politician, his main achievements were in relation to the navy, which he sought to improve in various ways during twenty years at the Admiralty. His reputation has suffered for a number of reasons. He was never personally very popular. He caught a good deal of blame, not really deserved, for the disastrous (from the British point of view) war in which the American colonies were lost. And later historians came to dislike what they took, again unjustifiably, to be his long term influence. Much remains to be explored about his career. He left some 19,000 letters and papers, many still not studied. However, Rodger is in no doubt that he did, in fact, father the sandwich, probably with salt beef, of which he was known to be fond. As he says, '…he has suffered the indignity of being forgotten as a man and remembered as a thing'.

History of the sandwich

However, it still does not seem entirely certain. Bread is one of the very earliest of foods, historically, and it is a fairly obvious idea to eat it with meat or cheese. A great many traditional diets include a substantial carbohydrate item, such as bread, pasta, rice, corn, potato, plus a smaller amount of protein – meat, fish, eggs, cheese. In the Middle Ages plates were often not used, food being eaten off thick pieces of bread called trenchers (French '*tranche*' a slice). A 'good trencherman' means a hearty eater. The trencher could of course be eaten as well. It would be a short step to putting some richer, tastier food between two slices. And long before that, Rabbi Hillel in the first century BCE is said to have devised a sandwich of two matzos with a filling of nuts, apple, spices, wine and bitter herbs, to be eaten at Passover.

Sandwiches are said to have reached America through a cookery book by the Englishwoman Elizabeth Leslie, who included ham sandwiches as a main course, in 1827. But again, no one can really be sure as to who first had the rather obvious thought. Sandwiches have proliferated, especially with the invention of commercial sliced bread. From about 1912 Otto Frederick Rohwedder of Iowa worked on inventing a bread slicer. He was told that sliced bread would go stale, so eventually added a wrapping device. Sliced, and wrapped, bread was, it seems, first offered by M.F. Bench's Chillicothe, Missouri, Baking Company in July 1928. We have much to thank America for.

There are histories of some of the more famous sandwich designs, such as the Club (chicken, bacon, tomato, lettuce, mayonnaise), and the Dagwood (multiple layers of bread plus any ingredient to taste, or to hand). But I shall not pursue them here. However, at the time of writing (June 2005) the present Earl of Sandwich, whose family firm sells sandwiches world-wide, is contesting the right to the name with the Earl of Sandwich Motel on route 6A in Cape Cod, USA.

41

SCHIZOPHRENIA MEANS A SPLIT PERSONALITY

as dramatically demonstrated in the story of Dr Jekyll and Mr Hyde, and films such as *The Three Faces of Eve* (1957), and *Sybil* (1973).

This confusion persists despite continual exhortations from experts and indeed patients and their families. It is made worse by the only partial understanding that we yet have of many psychological disorders.

'Split personality'
To take the 'split personality' first. This is not a generally recognised technical term. The popular implication is, of course, that one individual can somehow possess two, or more, 'personalities', which may alternate, as though there were two people in one body. Endless science fiction scenarios involve such switches. It is plausible to suggest that this is based on a dualist view of human beings, which was formulated influentially, though not originally, by the philosopher Rene Descartes (1596-1650). On this view, we consist of two parts, mental (or spiritual)

and physical. I am an entity who as it were lives in my body rather as I do in my house. All the evidence suggests that this is misleading. I am in fact a being who consists of all my attributes, physical, mental, emotional, spiritual and so on, which interact and work together to be me. None of them can exist separately from the others.

One of the features of such a being is awareness, and in particular self-awareness. We do not yet know how this human characteristic arises. Awareness, however, is never complete. At any moment, even when wide awake, there is much in our minds that we are not conscious of. But we can usually recall most of it if we want to. In some circumstances awareness can become restricted, and thoughts and memories become unavailable. This is often called 'dissociation'. An extreme case of this is the rare condition called a fugue state, in which a person, usually under stress, forgets who they are and adopts, usually temporarily, another 'personality'. Or more accurately, different aspects of their single personality. Some early investigators believed it was possible to switch between two or more such personalities, and left more or less dramatic accounts of this. R.L. Stevenson's Jekyll and Hyde are based on this, though he added the impossible feature that the body changed too, as seen in many a film version. It is now thought that such cases were at least partly induced, and exaggerated, by the investigators themselves. Nevertheless what is now called Dissociative Identity Disorder (DID) is accepted as a genuine condition. (This term replaces an earlier one, Multiple Personality Disorder or MPD.)

Schizophrenia
Schizophrenia is quite distinct, though even more tricky. The word was invented by the Swiss psychiatrist Eugen Bleuler in 1911, to refer to a group of patients with various symptoms, which he believed to be those of one illness. The symptoms included such things as hearing voices, feelings of being influenced by strange forces or other people, disorganised speech, writing and thinking, distorted awareness of reality, for example of time and place or self-identity (the origin of the popular 'man who thinks he is Napoleon'), inability to form or maintain normal

relationships with others, etc. Bleuler thought that the underlying cause was a breakdown in the basic mechanism of thinking, which at the time was generally held to be based on forming associations between ideas. Hence, schizophrenia, a 'split mind'.

The problem with this is that Bleuler really had no basis but his own observations and intuition. Since then, despite intensive studies, no single disease entity has been established – as it has, for example with malaria, influenza and a host of others. Patients are continually diagnosed as 'schizophrenic', but the word remains rather like 'ague' was in former times. Nowadays it is often said that this must have been malaria; but up to the late nineteenth century there was no reliable way of distinguishing the symptoms of malaria from those of rheumatic fever, severe influenza, and others.

In the 1960s, this led some psychiatrists such as R.D. Laing to proclaim that there was no such illness at all as schizophrenia. But this is just as misleading. Those diagnosed with it undoubtedly have more or less distressing symptoms. What we don't reliably know is why. It is also true that what seems to be a symptom in some societies or to some individuals, may not to others. Hearing voices, for example, may be experienced, and considered by others, as a genuine, if puzzling, communication from God or a devil.

The situation is well shown on the website of the (American) National Association of Mental Health on schizophrenia. This begins by stating baldly, 'Schizophrenia is a chronic, severe and disabling brain disease'. But later, it states that 'it may not be a single condition'. Thus, when studies report that 'schizophrenics' share a genetic characteristic, or brain abnormalities, or developmental traumas, one must remember that this means 'a particular group of patients who have been diagnosed as schizophrenic'. Whether they share the same illness cannot be stated certainly, as this is just what we are trying to find out.

Nevertheless, there is currently progress, and improved methods of treatment which can alleviate the symptoms. Curiously, one promising line shows that there may be a disorder of the neurotransmitters in the brain, so that perhaps Bleuler was partly on the right track.

However it turns out, it remains quite wrong to refer to those with these often severe symptoms as having a 'split personality', which implies two or more 'persons' functioning alternately. Rather, 'schizophrenic' symptoms involve a more or less complete breakdown of the normal personality, with consequent difficulties in functioning in normal life. It should also be stressed that this only very rarely means that the person is a danger to others. It is the exceptions that hit the headlines.

42

WE ALL REALLY HAVE SEVEN INTELLIGENCES

Though what this means, and how we know, perhaps few people could say.

'Seven intelligences' entered in an internet search engine yielded some 28,000 items. Most of the first 100, to go no further, state unequivocally that 'we' possess these. All attribute the idea, correctly, to the psychologist Howard Gardner (born 1943), and specifically to his book *Frames of Mind* (1983). He has developed the idea since then in many publications, and indeed has tried, apparently without much success, to dispel some of the myths that it has created. Like Frankenstein's creature, it has rather run amok. Gardner himself never expected the enthusiasm which it has created, especially among educationists and teachers.

What do you mean by 'intelligence'?

However, the idea itself can be criticised, on two main grounds. One is that it is a misleading use of terminology, and the other is that evidence is lacking. Gardner's 'intelligences' are, or were originally, linguistic, logical/mathematical, spatial, bodily/kinaesthetic, musical, interpersonal and intrapersonal. This was not meant to be a final list, and there is a case for spiritual intelligence, for example. The last two are more or less the 'emotional intelligence' made popular by Daniel Goleman in his book of that title (1995).

The problem with wording is that 'intelligence' has been used, by psychologists and general public alike, in many different ways. It has also come to be seen as a highly desirable quality. Scientists continually try to make their concepts, and the words that stand for them, more exact, whereas in common use words are often less precise. One of the most important tools of science is measurement. The science of measuring human characteristics is called psychometrics, which originates with the work of Sir Francis Galton (1822-1911). The measurement of human abilities rests on having people perform on a range of tasks, and correlating the results, that is, testing to see which go together. Thus, if one wanted to analyse athletic ability, one might get a large sample of people to perform the range of track and field events. Almost certainly, one would find that those who did well at one, tended to do well at others also. But they would also fall into more specialised groups, probably short races and long jump, longer races, high jump, and throwing events. This would give a general factor of athletic ability, and a number of sub-factors.

This is what has been found with intelligence. General cognitive ability, sometimes called 'g' for short, is a component of all intellectual performance, and then there are more specialised sub-abilities – in fact, the first three of Gardner's 'intelligences'. It is misleading, in my view, to call the whole list of seven, 'intelligences'. They are abilities; some cognitive, others less so. They are not discrete (as Gardner himself makes clear). But neither are they, as often seems to be thought, like so many little engines which we can switch on as required. Psychometric abilities, of which intelligence is one, are simply statements of what kinds of performance go together, based on measurement. We may then go further and investigate what underlies the performances, for example the functioning of the brain, and what factors favour development – genetic and environmental.

The 'seven intelligences' are not based on measurement. Two sorts of evidence are offered for them. The first is what is called 'localisation of function' in the brain, that is the identification of which bits of the brain are involved in which activities. The idea goes back at least as far as the now discredited attempts of phrenologists to assess abilities by feeling the alleged 'bumps' in the skull (which of course have no relation to the brain within). With modern methods, it can be done more reliably. But we are still a long way from knowing how the whole system works, and from what is known we cannot infer a fixed number of abilities (as, again, Gardner himself makes clear).

The range of human abilities

The other evidence is that different cultures value different sorts of ability. For example in the Middle Ages great value was placed on spirituality, whereas in our society (generally), more is attached to intellectual ability. Intelligence in the psychometric sense is closely related to success in education and careers, though of course it is far from the only factor. Part of the 'seven intelligences' message is that other sorts of ability ought to be valued also. And this is what has particularly appealed to educators.

Gardner's own definition of intelligence is: 'the capacity to solve problems, or to fashion products that are valued in more than one culture'. This is probably more like what most people would mean by 'intelligence', but scientifically it seems to me too general to be helpful. Even so, it is perhaps not general enough to include all that the 'seven intelligences' are often taken to mean. Can a sports player, for example, really be said to be solving problems or fashioning a product? Of course there is often an element of problem solving, particularly in positional games like snooker.

But most games depend far more on skill, and to call this a kind of intelligence is rather like calling a primrose a kind of shrub, rather than saying that both are varieties of plant. Biologists from Linnaeus on have provided a sound basis for classification.

Psychologists have always recognised that human beings have many and varied abilities, and have established fairly well how they relate to each other. There is value in most of them, though not all (some people excel at killing others). And we no doubt have not got to the end of them, and perhaps never will, as we constantly adapt to new conditions and to our own new inventions. Ability at computing did not exist a hundred years ago, though the general cognitive ability ('g') which it requires certainly did.

43

SHERLOCK HOLMES WORE A 'DEERSTALKER' HAT AND SMOKED A HOOK-SHAPED 'CALABASH' PIPE

and he lived with Dr Watson at 221B Baker Street in London, which can be visited today, or at least the site of it. Indeed he may be there still.

The adventures of Sherlock Holmes, the world's first consulting detective, are recounted in four long and fifty-six short stories by Sir Arthur Conan Doyle (1859-1930), published between 1887 and 1917.

The after-life of Sherlock Holmes
The character he invented has had probably the most extraordinary fate of any in fiction. A picture of a hawk-nosed

character, with the familiar hat and pipe, are used to advertise almost every conceivable product. Indeed these two objects alone convey 'detection' with no more information needed. As is well known, Holmes continues to receive several hundred letters every year. Many of these are from children, or cranks, or jokers. But some are from apparently serious persons who really think that the Great Detective can help them with their problem, whatever it may be. For years the letters were delivered to No 221 Baker Street, currently being rebuilt. 221B has never existed.

There are some hundreds of Sherlock Holmes societies all over the world, large and small. Likewise there are hundreds of books about Holmes, from scholarly studies to an ever-growing list of additional adventures by a host of authors. Holmes continues to feature also in every other possible medium – films, television, radio, comics, ballet, plays, songs, musicals ... you name it. In addition to the letter-writers, there is a kind of sub-genre of writing which rests on assuming that Conan Doyles' writings are the record of a real character, composed (mostly) by Dr John Watson – for whom Doyle is supposed to have acted as Literary Agent. I confess to having contributed one such book. The game then consists in explicating and glossing the Canon, as it is termed, and particularly in reconciling the many inconsistencies in it.

These actually arose because Doyle was quite careless about details in the stories. He considered them trivial beside his other literary work which is now largely forgotten, except for one other remarkable adventure tale, *The Lost World* (1911). This too has been the subject of numerous adaptations and variations, such as the '*Jurassic Park*' novels and films.

Where did Holmes and Watson live?
Doyle claimed, perhaps teasingly, that he had never been in Baker Street, which is and was a real street running north from Oxford Street. In any case, the section that now contains No. 221 was not then part of Baker Street, so that this cannot be where Holmes lived. And it does not fit Holmes's actions in the stories. Taking together all the clues in the Canon, the spot that best fits them is what is now No. 31, much further south. And if Holmes had lived

at the present 221, he could not still be there, because as all aficionados know, he retired finally and irrevocably to his cottage on the Sussex Downs, to keep bees and work on his still-awaited magnum opus, *The Whole Art of Detection*.

In the very first adventure, *A Study in Scarlet*, Holmes meets Watson and, being both single men with no settled home, they jointly rent the famous rooms. But in *The Sign of Four*, set a few years later, Watson meets Mary Morstan, subsequently marries her and sets up in a medical practice. Thereafter he mostly lives apart from Holmes, though visiting frequently.

As to the pipe and hat, the nearest Doyle gives us is a reference to a 'travelling cap', and to various pipes, indeed a 'litter' of pipes on the mantelpiece, including a briar, a clay and a long cherrywood – but no hook. Apparently this was introduced by the American actor William Gillette, who was the first to play Holmes on the stage, allegedly because he found it easier to speak with in his mouth. The cap was elaborated into a deerstalker in the original illustrations to the stories in *The Strand Magazine*. Actors playing Holmes usually adopt it, though in the substantial Granada TV series, Jeremy Brett mostly dressed, correctly, in the normal clothes of a gentleman of Holmes's day.

44

SIR FRANCIS CHICHESTER WAS THE FIRST MAN TO SAIL SINGLE-HANDED AROUND THE WORLD

as I have heard people say when admiring his yacht *Gypsy Moth IV* as she lies in dry-dock at Greenwich.

Indeed this claim is found on a tourist information website for Greenwich. Sir Francis was a remarkable man, but this feat was not his. Born in 1901, he went to New Zealand as a young man, and made a considerable fortune. This enabled him to achieve a series of feats in both airplanes and small boats. In 1960 he won the first solo race across the Atlantic. In 1966 he set off to sail single-handed around the world, in the 55-foot yawl *Gypsy Moth IV*. He returned after nine months and one day, 226 days sailing, and 29,600 miles. He was the first to do it with only one stop, at Sydney, Australia. The Queen had bestowed a knighthood on him while he was at sea, and signalised this in the ritual manner, a sword tap on the shoulder, at Greenwich. The sword is variously reported as the one with which Queen Elizabeth I had knighted Francis Drake, or alternatively the latter's own sword. The second Sir Francis made one more solo transatlantic voyage, and died in 1972.

Joshua Slocum

The honour of being first, however, belongs to the American mariner Joshua Slocum (1844-1909). Unlike Chichester he was a sailor all his life. At fourteen he ran away to sea in classic fashion. He returned, but left for good at sixteen. By 1869 he had his first command. In 1892 a friend, Captain Eben Pierce, gave him a 'ship' which 'needed some repairs'. It turned out to be a rotting old oyster boat propped up in a field, a 37-foot sloop (a single-masted vessel, whereas a yawl has two) named the Spray. Slocum rebuilt her himself, beginning by felling a nearby oak tree for a keel. Slocum points out that although effectively a new vessel, she was still the Spray. The cost was $553.62, and thirteen months hard work.

On 24 April 1895 Slocum set off in the Spray from Boston Harbour. His round the world route took him 46,000 miles (he crossed the Atlantic twice), and he returned, to Newport, Rhode Island, on 27 June 1898. His account of the epic trip, *Sailing Alone Round the World* (1900), was an instant best seller, It has been translated into many languages and is still in print. A first edition will cost you £100. Slocum was not, as many later voyagers have been, concerned about time, rather he wanted to see as much as possible. He continued sailing, but in 1909, aged 65, he left on a trip to South America, and was never heard from again.

Other solo voyagers

Between Slocum and Chichester another twenty-one solo voyages round the world were made, one man, Harry Pidgeon, doing it twice, though on the first occasion he took a short cut through the Panama Canal. The first Briton was John Guzzwell in 1959. In 1968-69 Robin Knox-Johnston and Bernard Moitessier both sailed single-handed and non-stop around the world. In 2005 Ellen MacArthur did it in 72 days.

Despite her obvious sea-worthiness, Francis Chichester disliked the *Gypsy Moth*, claiming that she was 'cantankerous and needs a crew of three – a man to navigate, an elephant to move the tiller, and a three foot six inch chimpanzee with arms eight feet long to get about below and work some of the gear'.

Records of solo round the world voyages are kept by the Joshua Slocum Society International, so if you are thinking of a little jaunt do let them know.

45

SLAVERY WAS INVENTED BY THE BRITISH, AND ENDED BY THE AMERICAN CIVIL WAR

and the (British) slave trade lasted for hundreds of years, causing the deaths of hundreds of millions of black Africans. And, Middle Eastern potentates have harems full of beautiful slave girls. And, Spartacus tried to end slavery in Ancient Rome.

A plaque by the Thames at Deptford in London about the slave trade mentions 'hundreds of years'. An article in *The Times* stated that 'hundreds of millions' of slaves died crossing the Atlantic. Hollywood films make the other items familiar. I have not actually seen it asserted that Britain invented slavery but mass media imply it.

The nature of slavery

Slavery seems to have existed as long as 'civilisation', if that is not contradictory. The first recorded code of laws, that of Hammurabi

(c. 3500 BCE) makes provision for slaves. It has probably been found in more societies than not. One might distinguish two forms, perhaps as 'primary' and 'secondary'. In many societies 'slavery' as a category of social organisation is, or has been, generally accepted and often enshrined in law. Such laws may make provision for how slaves should be treated, just as we commonly do for animals. But slaves are property as animals are.

In 'secondary' versions, slavery does not formally exist, but some people are treated in many ways *as if* they were slaves. They may be forced to work, often without payment, they may be controlled, or physically constrained, in what they can do or where they can go, they may effectively have no or very few rights. Slavery in this sense continues to the present day in many countries, as the society Anti-Slavery International amply documents. Slavery was expressly forbidden by the *United Nations Universal Declaration of Human Rights* in 1948, and by a further United Nations convention in 1956.

Slavery was an essential part of the economy of the Roman Empire. It has been estimated that perhaps 15-20% of the population were slaves. They were of course workers, many unskilled but also in many individual cases educated and even rising to important positions. They didn't, as films would have it, consist mainly of beautiful girls awaiting the whim of a rich man. The film harems, full of scantily clad starlets, likewise did not exist, harems being simply the female quarters of large households. Spartacus, familiar from the film starring Kirk Douglas, was a slave and a gladiator who led a revolt and, as a brilliant commander, scored some spectacular victories over Roman forces. But his aim was not, as in the film, to end slavery. Rather it was to escape it. His original plan seems to have been to lead his followers across the Alps into Gaul, but he turned back, and was eventually defeated and killed in battle in 72 BCE (not crucified as in the film).

Slavery, like many other institutions, including much of Roman law, survived the collapse of the Empire. It was accepted by the Christian Church. But gradually patterns changed. In Northern Europe in particular, the status of slave virtually died out, for various reasons. (A full account is given by Hugh Thomas in *The*

Slave Trade, 1997.) It persisted in Mediterranean countries, and it was endemic in Africa, with various roles being played by more and less aggressive tribes and powers, among the most influential being Islamic Arabs who came to dominate much of West African trade, including that in slaves.

The Slave Trade
The cross-Atlantic Slave Trade, which is what probably most people think of first, was begun by Portugal. In the fifteenth century Portuguese navigators boldly explored ever further, in particular down the West coast of Africa. Among the goods they brought back were African slaves, the first cargo being landed and sold in the Algarve in 1444. Portuguese sailors also colonised islands off Africa such as Madeira and the Canaries, and one of the uses of slaves there was in the cultivation of sugar cane. Much later this came to be a main occupation in the West Indies also. Other maritime countries, France, Spain, what is now Holland, and above all Britain, joined the exploration rush. The discredit of being the first British slave trader belongs to Sir John Hawkins, who set off in 1562 with the aim of taking slaves to Hispaniola. His enterprise was backed by numerous worthies including the Lord Mayor of London, although Queen Elizabeth expressed the pious if naïve hope that no Africans would be taken without their consent.

Between then and 1807, when the trade was abolished by Act of Parliament, British ships transported an estimated (by Thomas) 2,600,000 slaves across the Atlantic, out of a total of probably around eleven million. An estimate of losses en route may be around ten per cent overall, although on many voyages it was certainly greater. Although slaves were treated savagely, it was not in the interest of traders to lose their cargo. And the traders were mostly just that; they bought slaves in Africa, and sold them in the Americas. They did not create slaves, but they greatly increased the demand for them, and thus the numbers.

Britain was preceded in abolition by Holland, in 1805. The United States also outlawed the trade in 1807. The difference was, of course, that Britain and other European countries did not possess slave workers, whereas America was dependent on them, particularly in the Southern States. Thus it took another fifty years, and a violent war, to end the institution there.

46

SPARE THE ROD AND SPOIL THE CHILD
A belief held fiercely by some and vaguely by more.

In 1987 legislation was passed banning corporal punishment (CP) in British state schools. Opinion polls suggested that the move was widely unpopular. And despite continued campaigning, government has been consistently reluctant to ban it in the home. It seems that a majority of parents feel that they need to, or should, smack their children on occasion ('smack' is the usual term), though generally 'as a last resort'. Whether this is right is actually quite difficult to determine.

Does it work?

Taken literally, the saying is clearly nonsense. There are large numbers of children who have always been spared the rod, or any other instrument, and are manifestly quite unspoiled. It is much harder to tease out the actual effects of corporal punishment, especially long term. The biggest obstacle is that one cannot, for obvious reasons, do controlled experiments, in which various groups of children would receive various regimes, and then be followed up through life. Most longer term studies, when not merely anecdotal, have been retrospective, asking adults about their childhood. Such recollections are notoriously unreliable. Studies of short-term effects are more reliable, but cannot answer many important questions. And in any case, because experiments are impossible, studies are essentially correlational. What is shown is that CP is, or is not, associated with various effects. It is not certain that CP causes the effects. Further, it is often impossible to disentangle the effects of CP as such from various other aspects of child-rearing.

An extensive 'meta-analytic' study appeared in 2002 (by Elizabeth Thompson Gershon), putting together the results of eighty-eight investigations that were of sufficient standard. She concluded that CP is associated with eleven effects. One of these, short term compliance, was positive, the rest were negative. In other words, CP is effective in stopping children doing something they ought not to be doing (though that is not the same as getting them to do something better). In the longer term, it may (for example) increase aggressiveness, and delinquency, and may lead to poorer moral internalisation (self-control) and mental health. 'May' because these are correlations, not proved causal effects. Gershon is rightly cautious about conclusions, and this is reinforced by a group of critics led by Robert Lazelere, a defender of CP. They argue that bad results of CP are not due to the punishment itself, but to 'inept harsh parenting' with which it is often associated. The evidence, they say, does not justify banning it.

Is it right?

However, there are other ways of looking at it. What is corporal punishment? A widely accepted definition would be something like: 'the use of physical force with the intention of causing a child to experience pain but not injury for the purposes of correction or control of the child's behaviour' (Straus, 1994, quoted by Gershon). But where do you draw the line? Any physical force may cause injury, as sports players can testify. And what is pain – is it to include mental pain? One child may laugh off a smack, another be deeply hurt by sarcasm or rejection. One could argue that the real issue is not CP as such, but compulsion. However, physical force is always a manifestation of compulsion.

This leads to a further argument, that the issue is not really about effects but about morality, whether it is right to inflict pain. At one extreme are some religious devotees who take their stand (usually) on the Bible. It is sometimes asserted, indeed, that 'spare the rod, etc' is a direct quote, but it is not. The nearest things are from the Book of Proverbs: 'He that spareth his rod hateth his son, but he who loves him disciplines him diligently', and again '...withhold not correction from the child, for if thou shalt beat him with the rod he shall not die. Thou shalt beat him with the rod, and shalt deliver his soul from hell'. American web sites taking this line interpret 'rod' to mean 'paddle', the traditional American instrument (though one offers for sale a modern rod made from, I think, nylon). And they proclaim that disobedience, whether of child to parent or parent to God's word, 'is a SIN ... God *commands* us to spank with an implement', and so on. At the other extreme are those who either read the book quite differently, or reject the whole concept of a supernatural basis for morality.

Taking this line, it can be argued that compulsion, especially by physical force, is morally objectionable. It is up to the proponents of it to show clearly that there is no better alternative, and what good can be proved to come from it. And this has not been done. Further, many would say, what research does increasingly show is that right behaviour derives not from compulsion, except perhaps in the very short term, but from conditions in child-rearing, and in society generally, that foster, teach and reward it. This is not at all a woolly or soft-hearted approach, but a purely practical question of what actually works.

47

WE ONLY USE TEN PER CENT OF OUR BRAINS

...according to Albert Einstein, or William James. Or, as scientists have long known. Or, as psychologists have recently proved. Or, as ancient wisdom tells us. Etc., etc.

The claim appears all over the place. Uri Geller stated it in a radio programme (hardly a recommendation). A leaflet for L. Ron Hubbard's book *Dianetics* starts with it. One David Gray assures us, at www.experiencefestival.com, that 'A large number of scientific studies indicate that nearly all humans use no more than 15% of their inherent mental features'. And very often the conclusion is that therefore, if we only had access to the other ninety, or eighty-five, per cent, we could do all sorts of marvellous things. We could all be geniuses, or develop amazing psychic powers.

This particularly batty belief is about as sensible as saying we only use one of our fingers.

An absurd idea

Take first some commonsense points. First, any part of the body that is not used will atrophy. This is seen in those unfortunate to suffer paralysis of some part of the body, and also in some religious devotees who deliberately refrain from using one limb, sometimes for years. But apart from disease, the brain does not atrophy, as most of it should if it really were not used. Second, the brain, like the rest of us, has evolved over millennia as a result of the functions it has. How could the unused ninety per cent have survived the selective process of evolution? It would have disappeared like the tails we no longer need. Third, non-fatal specific damage can occur to any part of the brain from accidents. Getting something pushed through the brain, a bullet, a nail or whatever, always results in impaired functioning, at least to some extent. But by chance, most of such traumas ought to fall in the large unused part, if it existed, and have little or no effect on what the brain does.

But there are many scientific facts as well that disprove the thing. The activity of the brain can be monitored continuously and in great detail, using such techniques as positive emission tomography (PET scanning). This shows that the whole brain is more or less active all the time, though activity is greatest in particular areas corresponding to what is being done. This localisation of function, as it is known, itself demonstrates the fallacy. We need all the parts of the brain to carry out all we do, from basic functions like breathing, walking and eating, to solving complex problems.

Origins of the idea

Much more evidence is summarised by Barry Beyerstein (in *Mind Myths*, edited by Sergio Della Sala, published by Wiley, 1999). He also tried to find the origins of the notion, but could not, after extensive searching. It was certainly around in the early part of the last century, but where it came from originally is a mystery. As mentioned above, it is often attributed, arbitrarily, to some revered authority such as Albert Einstein, or William James, the father of American psychology. Of course invocation of a prestigious name is an ancient way of gaining acceptance. And it is almost impossible to prove that the person quoted did not, at some time, say something like what is alleged, possibly taken out of context. But no eminent scientist, least of all a psychologist, could seriously put forward the idea that is now popularly presented.

Beyerstein argues that the idea arose and persisted in a context of belief in self-improvement, with considerable overtones of the occult and 'New Age' ideas. But quite why these themselves have been so widespread, and why the particular 'ten per cent of the brain' idea caught on, remain to be explained.

48

THE *TITANIC* WAS CONSIDERED TO BE UNSINKABLE BEFORE HITTING THE FAMOUS ICEBERG

Nearly all those on board lost their lives, and this was the greatest ever maritime disaster.

The loss of the *SS Titanic* is almost certainly the most famous story of disaster at sea, re-told in books and particularly in spectacular films. There seems to be an unquenchable public appetite for pictures of people losing their lives. The basic facts are that the ship was launched on 31st May 1911, and set out from Southampton on her maiden voyage on 10th April 1912. On 14th April she struck an iceberg, and sank the following day. There were 3,547 people on board, of whom approximately 1,500 were lost (about 43%). The tragedy immediately attracted intense interest, and anything to do with it, such as the recovery of items from the wreck, or the personal lives of survivors, is still hot news.

Was she 'unsinkable?'

All sorts of tales circulated, such as that of the band which supposedly played on until the actual moment of sinking. Among them was the idea that the ship had been considered to be, and stated to be, 'unsinkable', and that the loss was therefore a kind of warning against human pride, humbled by the forces of nature. Certainly the *Titanic* was in 1912 the largest ship in the world, and was advertised as both the safest and the most luxurious.

The builders, Harland and Wolff, always claimed that they never described her as 'unsinkable'. Indeed it is unlikely that any major shipbuilding firm would ever make such a really wild statement. They better than anyone would know that no ship can be completely immune to accidents. However, a brochure issued in 1910 by the owners, the White Star Line, about the two proposed sister ships, the *Titanic* and the *Olympic*, did say that they were 'designed to be unsinkable'. At the time of her launch the *Irish News and Belfast Morning News* described the ship as 'practically unsinkable'. This phrase was also used by the *Shipbuilder Magazine* in 1911. And later, after the tragedy, at least two passengers who survived stated that they had heard, or had thought, that she was 'unsinkable', and indeed that this influenced them to undertake the voyage.

For whatever reasons, the loss of the *Titanic* has come to seem a kind of archetype of maritime tragedy, the case always quoted, and at the same time assumed to be the worst. In April 2004, for example, in the course of reporting the arrival of the *Queen Mary 2* in New York, *The Times* referred to the *Titanic* as 'the worst maritime disaster in history'. Presumably 'worst' is to be taken in terms of numbers of lives lost. A correspondent, Mr Brian Turvey, pointed to the loss of the *Wilhelm Gustloff*, a commandeered cruise ship which in 1945 was bringing German refugees to safety across the Baltic Sea. On 30th January she was sunk by a Russian submarine, the *S-13*. How many were on board was not exactly recorded, but estimates of the number lost vary from 5,900 to 7,000.

Tragedies at sea

In fact, the International Registry of Sunken Ships gives details of twenty-two cases in which more than 1600 lives were lost. The five worst cases all occurred during the Second World War. There is some uncertainty as to exact numbers, often because the ships were carrying refugees who had obviously been crammed on board with little regard for counting, or indeed safety. In April 1945 the *Goya*, another German ship, was sunk by another Russian submarine, the *L-3*. Some 6,200 lives were lost. Then there was the *Junyo Maru*, sunk by the American submarine *USS Sturgeon*, on 18th September 1944. Around 5,400 were drowned, though another 600 were picked up by escort vessels. The *Cap Arcona* was yet another German vessel in the Baltic, sunk this time by British aircraft with the loss of between five and seven thousand. Earlier in the war the *Lancastrian*, a British ship, was sunk on 17th June 1940 by German aircraft, with a loss of between 3,000 and 4,500. Some accounts put it as high as 7,000. The official British report into this disaster will not be published until the year 2040, for what reason one can only guess.

In general, natural disasters such as famine, plague, earthquakes, drought and floods far excel even the most enthusiastic efforts of the human race to destroy other human beings. But at sea, it is human action that must be held responsible for the worst disasters. However, another letter to *The Times*, from Mr W.B. Simpson, mentioned what was perhaps a combination of the two, when in 1281 Kublai Khan made his second attempt to invade Japan. Almost all the 4,400 ships of his invasion fleet were wrecked by a *kamikaze* or 'divine wind'. Scores of thousands of Chinese, Mongolian and Korean soldiers and sailors perished.

49

TOBACCO WAS INTRODUCED INTO ENGLAND BY SIR WALTER RALEIGH

and he had a bucket of water thrown over him when a servant saw him smoking. Or it may have been a mug of ale.

That at least is the story I recall from early years. It may have come to me from *The Children's Encyclopaedia*, a fascinating and stimulating work in eight volumes which I read avidly. Later I discovered it was not always quite as accurate or objective as it might have been.

How we got tobacco
Tobacco is the name for the several varieties of *nicotiana*, nearly all native to the Americas. Columbus in 1492 found the natives of what are now the West Indies (because of course he thought he

had reached India) using it, and apparently brought back some leaves and seeds to Europe. It was slow to catch on. But it is recorded in France in 1556, in Portugal in 1558, in Spain in 1559, and in England in 1565, when it was apparently grown, on a small scale. *Nicotiana*, and nicotine, come from Jean Nicot, a French ambassador to Portugal.

The fate of Raleigh

Sir Walter Raleigh (1554?-1618) was one of the most flamboyant figures of a flamboyant age. A brilliant seaman, he was handsome and dashing as a young man and became a favourite of Queen Elizabeth, who showered property and privilege on him. It seems unclear whether there is any truth in the other well-known tale of Raleigh, that he laid his cloak over a puddle so that the Queen could keep her feet dry. Full of enterprises, some of which succeeded and some not, such as an expedition to Guiana in search of the fabled gold mines of El Dorado, he fell out of favour largely due to secretly courting, and then marrying, one of the Queen's ladies in waiting. Before that, however, he had persuaded Elizabeth to try tobacco, and become a regular smoker of it himself. It was long thought to have therapeutic qualities, like another New World import, quinine (which did).

However, although he made several adventurous voyages, Raleigh never visited Virginia, which was the main source of tobacco. The connection between him and the drug seems largely due to Thomas Harriot (1560-1621). Harriot was an outstanding mathematician and astronomer, whom as a young man Raleigh took into his household, initially as mathematical tutor. Harriot put his learning to practical use and made several contributions to the development of navigation. Raleigh sent him on one of his enterprises to Virginia, as a surveyor. It is said that he brought back some of the clay pipes that the natives used for smoking, though Raleigh himself often used a silver one. In 1588 Harriot published *A Brief and True Report of Virginia*, in which he described both tobacco and the potato.

Raleigh's contribution was that he was perhaps the first Englishman of note to be a regular smoker. He made it fashionable, in fact. It is easy to see how the legend about introducing it could have arisen. Legends, particularly of origins, tend to get attached to any well-known and more or less plausible name. The bucket of water, or mug of ale, was perhaps simply the humorous invention of some story-teller. Sadly, both Raleigh and Harriot came to unfortunate ends. Raleigh fell foul of James I after he succeeded in 1603, was put in the Tower of London, and eventually beheaded for treason on extremely flimsy evidence. James, with more justification as it turned out, also detested tobacco and wrote a famous diatribe against it. As for Harriot, he died of cancer, of the nose. Whether this was due to tobacco, possibly in the form of snuff, is unknown. In any case, diagnoses were still largely a matter of guesswork at that time.

50

ANCIENT TOMBS ARE GUARDED BY FIENDISHLY INGENIOUS BOOBY-TRAPS

which work perfectly no matter how old they are, and which can be negotiated only by our intrepid hero, usually to find a fabulous treasure.

This notion appears in endless films, stories and computer games, such as the box office smash 'Indiana Jones' adventures, notably the first, *Raiders of the Lost Ark* (1981), which begins with just such events. The booby-traps are perhaps most often mechanical, involving stepping on the wrong paving stone, or lifting the treasure from its age-old resting place, thus setting off a fall of stones, or opening of a pit, or spears shooting out from walls, or other ingenious device. Sometimes the penalty includes dangerous snakes or scorpions, which have apparently lived for centuries in anticipation of this moment. (In much the same way, caverns and tunnels are usually equipped with ever-burning torches for the use of the adventurer.)

But sometimes the trap has a supernatural element, and can be circumvented by spiritual means, such as self-belief, or by some magical process or charm. Such perils also occur in many a science fiction adventure.

Real-life tombs
I have been unable to find any authentic case of such a trap in real life, though that does not prove they have never existed. I have visited an underground prehistoric chamber in Malta, the descending entry to which has a sudden unexpected twist, which was alleged to be designed to trick unwanted intruders, though there were no moving parts. It is difficult to imagine what kind of mechanism, particularly as elaborate as Indiana Jones for one encounters, could possibly survive in working order for many centuries, without the slightest maintenance.

The questions seem to be, not so much whether they exist, as where the idea comes from, and why it is so popular. The simplest answer to the second is that is just makes a good adventure, a change from a human adversary. And certainly the basic theme of a hero braving dangers to retrieve a hidden treasure is as old, in all probability, as story-telling itself. That the treasure should be in a tomb may simply derive from the fact that peoples all over the world have indeed interred valuable artifacts, 'grave goods', with their dead. It is assumed that this is due to a belief in life after death, even in pre-history. When records are available, as in ancient Egypt above all, we know that this is indeed the case. It is hardly necessary to say that there is no evidence whatever to support the idea of life after death, and never has been. That it is nevertheless one of the most dearly held beliefs is consistent with an extremely strong evolutionary urge to survival. All living things, and above all humans, fight for life in almost all circumstances, and those that do so best will necessarily have the greatest chance of having descendants.

Egyptian provision for the dead, at least the wealthy and powerful, was particularly elaborate, although the concept of what happened in the otherworld seems to have been less precise. The result was, however, that the vast majority of tombs were robbed, often quite soon after being sealed. The famous tomb of Tutankhamun, discovered in 1922, was a rare exception – and not a particularly grand one by ancient standards. The boy Pharaoh seems to have died suddenly and been placed in a tomb intended for one of humbler station. In many other countries too, robbing has been the norm until recent times, and is still practiced. Thus the treasure part of the myth has a very real basis.

Why booby-traps?

The booby-trap idea is harder to account for. The following are only suggestions. First, there is the superstitious fear of the dead, who might wreak revenge on molesters. Just such stories cluster around the story of the Tutankhamun tomb, and many others. Second, there would very often be real danger in entering tombs, especially large ones which might collapse at any moment. Third, presumably to deter robbers, Egyptian tombs, at least, often contained narrow passages and strongly sealed doors, difficult to negotiate.

Fourth, I suggest that the ancient booby-trap may have its fictional origin in Henry Rider Haggard's best-selling novel *King Solomon's Mines* (1885). The setting is not a tomb it is true, but the eponymous diamond mines. But the treasure chamber is concealed behind a massive thirty ton stone, which opens when a hidden lever is pulled. The narrator, Haggard's hero Alan Quartermaine, suggests it is counterbalanced like a sash window. The secret is known only to the unbelievably ancient witch Gagool, who traps the adventurers inside, but fails to slip back under the slab and is crushed. She has first stabbed the beautiful and noble black girl Foulata, rather to the relief of Quartermaine/ Haggard, since she is in love with one of the party, Captain Good, RN, and such an entanglement would of course be quite unsuitable. There are no convenient everlasting torches, but with the help of eight matches they eventually escape. But they can never find the way back in, the secret being now 'utterly lost...It was certainly a marvellous bit of mechanism, characteristic, in its massive and yet inscrutable simplicity, of the age which produced it; and I doubt if the world has such another to show'.

More generally, I have speculated that the notion of ancient, hidden, but still active mechanisms became for some reason a commonplace of the late nineteenth century. It pervades the work not only of romancers such as Rider Haggard, but such unlikely authors as Conan Doyle and Sigmund Freud. Anyone interested might look at my *The Intelligence of Sherlock Holmes and Other Three-Pipe Problems* (1999).

51

UNIVERSITIES WERE ORIGINALLY RELIGIOUS FOUNDATIONS FOR TRAINING PRIESTS

and they were communities of impractical scholars pursuing learning for its own sake. And they existed to give aristocrats the education of a gentleman.

These ideas are not consistent with each other. But inconsistency has seldom bothered those of fixed beliefs. Of course, if like Mr Charles Clarke, Secretary of State for Education(!) in 2003, you consider that mediaeval history is merely 'ornamental', it doesn't matter much. It is of course axiomatic in the British style of government that those in charge of anything should know nothing about it. It would only prejudice them.

How universities began

However. The origins of Western universities are complex, but the main points are well established. Let us mention three major factors. One was the revival of civic life in the twelfth century, particularly in Italy, where it had never entirely died out with the collapse of Roman rule. This created a need for professionals, especially lawyers and doctors. One was the development of schools, secular not religious, though often centred on cathedrals and large churches. And one was, indeed, the need of the Church for trained theologians.

Some claim that the first university was the medical school at Salerno in Sicily, but most authorities give the title to Bologna. Although later than Salerno, it came to have the features that distinguished mediaeval universities, and has had a continuous existence. It began with the teaching of law in the twelfth century, particularly by the distinguished jurist Irnerius. Organisation developed gradually, originally student-based. Students hired masters to teach them. This pattern was followed elsewhere. A vestige of it remains in the election of a Rector by the students in some Scottish universities, and an echo of it in the American 'Greek letter' societies.

The second and third universities to emerge, Paris and Oxford, adopted rule by masters, which eventually became the norm. Both arose in the same spontaneous way as Bologna, as did other early examples in Italy, Reggio, Vincenza, Arezzo and the most successful, Padua. In Spain and Portugal, on the other hand, the first universities were created by sovereigns of the various states which then existed. Palencia was the first to be certainly so founded, by King Alfonso VIII of Castile in 1208. Even so, it was based on an older episcopal school. Although the Church did not originally create universities (though it did later), it was not slow to try to control them.

Oxford came formally into existence in 1214, arising from a dispute between Town and Gown. Two students were hanged by the civic authorities, and the Papal Legate, Nicholas de Romanis, stepped in. He gave the Bishop of Lincoln authority to appoint a Chancellor to keep things in order. In the course of many years, the Chancellor became an honorary head of the University, delegating his powers to a deputy, which is why English universities title their chief executive, Vice-Chancellor. In other cases a sovereign obtained Church authority. In Prague King Charles IV of Bohemia sought a Papal Bull of foundation before issuing an imperial charter (1347), for the university which still bears his name.

What the first universities taught

The general pattern of study that developed began with the basic Arts degree, largely what we might call 'transferable skills'. 'Grammar', for example, was Latin, the common language of diplomacy, administration and scholarship. 'Rhetoric' was persuasive communication; 'Dialectic' was logic and reasoning. Students who wished, and were able, went on to one of the three 'higher faculties' in law, medicine or theology.

Universities were, in fact, professional training schools. Some taught other professional skills such as accountancy, though not for degrees. Some dons were no doubt, as ever, 'remote and ineffectual' as Belloc had it. Some were devoted to scholarship and learning. But in general, A.D. Cobban (*The Mediaeval Universities*, 1975) describes 'the rigorous, exacting nature of the academic courses designed to equip graduates to deal with the empirical and physical problems of living and of society', which might well be emulated today.

Students were in general what we would call 'upwardly mobile'; boys (no girls of course) of the middle or lower classes who wanted to better themselves. Many were quite poor and sometimes worked as servants to the better off. They would have learned their necessary Latin at free public schools founded by benefactors or run by the Church. It is true that in later centuries, at least in England, the only two universities, Oxford and Cambridge, came to be more associated with the wealthy classes, though never entirely so. And in the eighteenth century they reached rather a low point intellectually, with notable exceptions. They had also lost much of their professional emphasis. There was still a connection with the official Church of England, but this was no longer universal, rather a branch of the state and a sort of social service. Numbers of students did then seek mainly a modicum of education and good manners which would fit them for the life of a gentleman. But this was a far cry from what universities had originally been.

If I were to suggest one watchword for today's universities, it would be 'professionalism' – both for their own practice and for the students they seek to produce. But current political policies in the UK are, alas, diametrically opposed to such an aim.

52

WALES IS THE LAND OF SONG, AND THE WELSH ARE UNUSUALLY MUSICAL,

whereas the English are unmusical, which is why England has been called 'the land without music'. And a few other musical notions.

'The land of song' has become a catchphrase, enthusiastically promoted by the Welsh tourist board. One gets the impression that one can hardly walk down a Welsh street without being half drowned in a sea of music. I can't say that I have ever noticed it, on numerous visits. Of course there are several strong traditions of music making in Wales. One is that of choral singing, especially male voice choirs. This takes a more informal shape with the massed singing at Rugby and football matches. Another is for *eistedfoddau*, organised celebrations of, especially, traditional and folk music, often with a competitive component. The most famous is no doubt the International Eisteddfod at Llangollen in Denbighshire, which takes place in July each year. It was here, curiously enough, that Luciano Pavarotti made his international debut – in a male voice choir.

Music in Wales

Of course everyone has heard of a 'Welsh harp', though perhaps most people confuse it with a concert harp played by a Welsh person. The true Welsh harp is much smaller, with triple 'sympathetic' strings. It is, among other things, the traditional instrument for *penillion* singing, in which two people sing to a harp, or nowadays another instrument, played by one of them, according to various rules.

Wales has also strong traditions of classical music, with active orchestras and opera companies, and has produced many fine singers, instrumentalists, conductors and composers. And of course there is Tom Jones, who speaks with a delightful Welsh lilt but sings in dreary mid-Atlantic. But one cannot conclude that the Welsh people are naturally more musically gifted than any other group. No one seems to have tried to measure the amount, or quality, of music made by any particular society, and compare it with others. On the other hand, cultures do clearly vary in their attitudes to music as to other practices. Some strongly encourage it, others do not. In extreme cases it has been forbidden entirely, usually for religious reasons, or permitted only to a very limited degree.

Music is universal

All human groups, as far as we know, have produced music. It has been suggested (by Steven Mithen) that it may even have preceded speech. But it has different forms and functions in different circumstances. In our society, Western classical music has attained the highest prestige, and its norms have come to seem the standard against which other music should be assessed. Its origins have largely been first for religious purposes, and then for the entertainment of an aristocratic leisured class. As such it has largely been the work of professionals.

But this is very untypical of many other societies, in which music has been a more or less spontaneous outcome of communal activity, such as rituals and festivals, small group interaction, or even war. This is not to say that practitioners in such milieus have not often been highly skilled and deliberately trained. Examples of this are the Scottish tradition of *piobaireachd*, the 'great music' of the pipes, Indian and Chinese traditions, the Irish traditions such as sean nos singing, epic ballad singing in many societies, etc. More recently, pop and rock music emerged as in many ways a new kind of folk music, played, as the Beatles originally did, by local musicians for a local dance hall audience, though rather quickly becoming commercialised. In the UK, pop, rock and closely related forms account for some 90% of sales; classical for 3.5%, jazz 2%, while other varieties make up the rest. This dominance is bound to affect the whole pattern of musical life. It is reported that in Italy, the traditional home of opera, it is becoming impossible to find potential singers, as young people only want pop.

In the nineteenth century the idea gained currency that England was a 'land without music', possibly because it did not seem to be producing great composers in the classical tradition. In fact there were many musical activities. Not only a strong classical orchestral tradition, but such things as brass bands, music hall, oratorio, light opera, and the village bands described in the novels of Thomas Hardy. Virtually unknown to the intelligentsia was the vast rich body of folk music, which was the common culture of a society without mass media or recording.

Like all human attributes, music must be the outcome of both genetic and cultural factors. Recently a study of twins (one of the standard methods of teasing out this interaction) has concluded that tone deafness owes some 80% to genetic inheritance. The implication is that musical ability, or at least potential, also has a strong genetic component, though this has yet to be demonstrated. All human abilities so far investigated show this. Tone deafness affects about one in twenty of the population. At the other end of the scale is 'perfect pitch', which is known to run in families. But it is not, as is often supposed, a peculiar all-or nothing gift. Sensitivity to pitch is distributed in the population like other traits, and can be improved by training.

It is conceivable that the Welsh are genetically endowed with extra musical ability, and the English with less. But it is very unlikely. It is however reasonable to say that how this ability is manifested, in any human group, will vary according to the rules, customs and fashions of that group.

53

WITCHES ARE STRANGE WOMEN WHO WEAR POINTED BLACK HATS AND RIDE THROUGH THE AIR ON BROOMSTICKS,

they stir cauldrons full of potions and put curses on people, whom they can turn into toads or what they will. And much more.

Witches have had such a generally bad press that it is hard to know where to begin. Harry Potter hasn't helped. J.K. Rowling's books about the young wizard have made her by a very long way the most financially successful author who has ever lived. She must be doing something right, but her account of magic and wizardry is pretty much the stuff of folktales and fantasy, including such old favourites as magic wands and broomsticks.

What are witches?

Part of the problem is that 'witches' appear in many contexts and many guises. A simple point is that there is no connection between being a witch and being a woman. Witches in all contexts are both male and female. It is sometimes said that a male witch is a 'warlock' but this is just another word for a sorcerer, or sometimes a deceiver. Witches come to public attention in several ways. Apart from the fanciful version perpetuated in stories and films, perhaps the main ones are, the witch persecution craze of the early modern period, the current neopagan 'Wiccan' religions, and related to both, various theories about what witches were originally. There are also contemporary beliefs in witchcraft in various societies. There is often a confusion here with 'witch doctors', again largely due to fictional accounts of curses wrought by such figures, in films usually with a lot of leaping about and waving of sticks. The function of witch doctors, in societies that support them, is to combat the harm supposedly done by witches, such as illnesses or other misfortunes. It is a natural tendency, in the absence of a scientific explanation, to attribute such harm not to chance but to malevolence on the part of an enemy.

Persecution

A belief in witchcraft, whether benign or harmful, has generally been endemic, accepted in the same sort of way that we accept the possibility of getting a cold or flu. But at times it has flared up, resulting in waves of irrational persecution. These are much like the sudden accession of hatred towards other minorities such as Jews, gypsies or homosexuals. The witch craze in Europe lasted from the fifteenth to the eighteenth centuries, but was really virulent from about 1550 to 1650. A famous episode in the late seventeenth century was at Salem in Massachusetts, when nineteen supposed witches were hanged. The numbers in Europe were much greater, though they have often been exaggerated. Recent estimates suggest that up to forty or fifty thousand met their deaths.

The causes of this persecution are not fully understood, but some features appear to stand out. Supposed witches were very varied, and seem to have no features in common. Moreover outbreaks were both sporadic and localised, and similarly followed no general pattern. However, there was in many cases a preponderance of women, who tended to be old, alone and isolated from the community. Women, of course, have always outlived men. The folklore image of the witch, long pointed nose and chin, is that of an old person who has lost their teeth.

The idea of witchcraft, and attacks on witches, were normally opposed by both Church and State (and not, as is sometimes supposed, promoted by the Inquisition.). Outbreaks tended to occur where both these forces were weak, especially in Germany, Switzerland and eastern France, when the Reformation had destroyed much of the old certainty of mediaeval Europe. Part of this was a form of what would now be called social service. The Church did provide ways of accommodating and supporting the elderly and isolated. Nothing more natural, perhaps, than that a poor old woman, lacking traditional sources of help, should mutter 'curses' against seemingly selfish neighbours, which might be remembered when illness struck or crops failed. Flying is a very common dream, possibly mixed up with reality now and then by confused old people. Broomsticks were common enough, but the connection with flying is obscure. It goes back at least to Roman times, and one suggestion is that a broom handle was used as a masturbation aid, possibly with 'witches' ointment' which might have contained hallucinogenic agents.

Modern witches

Two attempts to reinterpret the craze have influenced modern witches. The first was that of Margaret Murray (1863-1963), an Egyptologist who in 1921 proposed that the persecuted witches were in fact practitioners of an ancient religion dating from neolithic times, and surviving underground through the Christian centuries. No reputable scholar accepts her case, which was based on partial and misread, and at times distorted, evidence. The other line has been that the 'witches' were healers and 'wise women', who were persecuted by male society, particularly with the rise of medicine as a male dominated, and much more sophisticated, profession. There is even less evidence for this. It is possible that some elements of traditional folk medicine and folklore survived over long periods, just as some songs and traditions have done, or at least the underlying themes. (Sir Eric Hobsbawm the historian used to claim that in a remote part of Italy he had come across a shrine to Saint Venus.)

However, those who now use the title 'wiccans' have evolved a set of beliefs that draw on many sources, some of them channeled through, or possibly invented in, the writings of Gerald Gardiner (1884-1964) in the late 1940s, including Celtic, Masonic and ceremonial magic traditions. They may believe variously in one, two, many or no deities, but in general emphasise respect and love for nature and other beings, celebrated in seasonal rituals. Spells are used, but only for good. They have nothing to do with Satanism, a derivative of Christianity which is equally rejected, at least in its hardline forms. Wiccan groups are said to be widespread in the USA, but to keep mostly out of sight from a (justified) fear of persecution.

Currently, amid a breakdown of law and order, the endemic belief in witchcraft in Africa is spawning an epidemic of persecution of supposed witches, for example in the Democratic Republic of Congo, particularly appalling as it is largely directed against children.

54

THE WRIGHT BROTHERS BUILT THE FIRST HEAVIER-THAN-AIR FLYING MACHINE
and made the first flight, on 17th December 1903, at Kitty Hawke, North Carolina

Like so many breakthroughs, the Wright brothers' flight arose in the context of partially successful attempts to do the same thing. The first successful attempts to rise from the earth used the lighter-than-air approach, a balloon in fact. The first recorded hot air balloon ascent was in 1709, by Bartolomeu de Gusmao. It was done indoors. The first manned flight is credited to Jean Francois Pilatre de Rozier and the Marquis Francois Laurent d'Arlandes, who toured six miles around Paris in 1783, in a Montgolfier hot air balloon.

The first aviator?

The line that eventually led to today's aviation had an earlier origin. Kites were developed in China from around 400 BC, and were the forerunners of gliders. But these had to wait until the time of the industrial revolution. Sir George Cayley (1773-1857), a forgotten pioneer in several fields, developed gliders so successfully that one was able to carry a boy of ten some distance, in 1849. This young hero, about whom nothing seems to be recorded, can be seen as the first aviator in the line that leads directly to today's astronauts. In 1853 Cayley sent his coachman aloft, but the latter promptly resigned, claiming he had been hired to drive, not fly. Cayley moreover envisaged the use of airships, helicopters, airplanes and even vertical take-off, and worked out many of the principles that would ultimately make manned flight possible, as the Wright brothers later acknowledged. He correctly saw that four factors must be balanced to achieve flight: lift, thrust, drag and gravity. But he had in particular no means of attaining suitable thrust, that is an engine simultaneously powerful and light in weight. Gliders, however, were developed further. One by Otto Lilienthal in 1891 could carry a person for long distances. His 1889 book on flight was used by the Wright brothers.

Powered flight

The brothers were also given, as boys in 1878, one of the 'bats' invented by Alphonse Penaud. He thought the bat a suitable design for a flying machine, but he called his invention a 'planophone'. It had an eighteen inch wing span, and an eight inch pusher propeller. This was powered by a rubber cord – another of George Cayley's ideas. In 1876 Alphonse Penaud took out a patent for a steam-powered human-carrying plane. But lack of success and increasing disability (he had early on suffered a serious injury to his hip) led him to commit suicide in 1880, aged only thirty. He was followed by Clement Ader, like the Wright brothers a maker of bicycles, and an inventor with fifty-eight patents to his name. He created a steam-powered model, the *Eole* (from Aeolus the god of the winds), which was launched down a runway. It rose to a height of one foot and flew for 165 feet. This led the French government to fund the development of a full-size machine for military use. But the twin-engined *Avion III* made only one, unsuccessful, flight, and was abandoned. Its name, avion, however, was officially adopted as the French for flying machine.

Similarly, in 1891 Samuel P. Langley made a steam-powered model plane that flew for three quarters of a mile. He embarked on a full-scale version, but it turned out to be too heavy for the power available, and crashed on the first attempted flight. Langley lost interest in the project. One last pre-Wright effort of note was that of Sir Hiram Maxim, an American who adopted British nationality, and made a large fortune from his Maxim machine gun. He built an enormous machine, a test rig, with a wing area of 4000 square feet, and two steam engines driving two 17 feet propellers. It ran on an 1800 feet rail track, carrying a pilot. It was not intended to take off, but on 31st July 1894, with Maxim at the controls, it did so for a few moments. Maxim, however, cut the power and the flight ended. He subsequently abandoned the project.

There may even have been other, unrecorded, efforts. The Reverend Burrell Cannon of Pittsburg, North Texas, inspired by a passage in the book of Ezekiel which seems to mention flying, constructed a human-carrying machine which may, or may not, have risen from the ground in 1902. Cannon was secretive about his project for fear of spies, and the machine was later lost.

Wilbur (1867-1912) and Orville (1871-1948) Wright based their efforts on all the recognised work that had already been done. They read all that was available, and corresponded with some of the pioneers. But they also made crucial innovations, including the use of a petrol engine. And they indisputably created the first successful airplane. They took it in turns to be pilot, and on 17th December 1903 it was Orville's turn. He flew for 120 feet, and as they say the rest is history. But the brothers did not, strictly, make the first heavier-than-air flying machine, nor the first flight in one.

193

55

YOU CANNOT PROVE A NEGATIVE
And its close relative, 'absence of evidence is not evidence of absence'.

These are, unlike most of the items in this collection, really matters of argument rather than of fact. But they are frequently asserted. And rather often in a context of disputes about religion, which I have on the whole avoided. However the principles are general and not at all tied to such disputes.

Negatives proved
It is obvious at once that you can prove a negative. 'I am not six feet tall' can be proved by anyone who cares to come round with

a tape measure. Logical proofs can be negative, say for example 'All swans are white; this bird is black; therefore this bird is not a swan'. Similarly with mathematical proofs: 'Two and two do not equal five', or indeed six or any number but four, because that is how the numbers are defined. Four is that which is the sum of two and two. The difficulty arises with empirical questions, like my height, but which cannot be readily checked with a tape measure. This may be because the means of measuring or observing do not exist. Formerly, it was not possible to prove that the moon was not made of green cheese, unlikely as it might seem (and even more so to me for years, until I learned that 'green' cheese is new cheese, generally white in colour). But now, of course, men have been there, and brought bits back, and it isn't. Or the proof requires observations so extensive that they are in practice, or even in principle, impossible. 'Three-headed pink unicorns do not exist' is impossible to test exhaustively as we cannot reach all parts of the universe, and as yet do not even know the extent of it, or whether there are others universes as well.

Absence of proof and proof of absence

Nevertheless most people would probably accept that it is reasonable to assume the non-existence of this particular breed of unicorn, even though it cannot be absolutely proved. Especially since there is no record of a unicorn of any kind ever having been found. So it is with God, who gets into the act sooner or later. Religious apologists assert that one cannot prove he does not exist. And non-believers often hesitate to say they are atheists, not wishing to assert something dogmatically about which they cannot be absolutely certain. They usually would say, however, that there is no proof that God does exist either.

Here we can call in an expert witness, Dr David Jenkins, former Bishop of Durham. In his book *The Calling of a Cuckoo* (2002), a kind of spiritual autobiography, Dr Jenkins tells how as a child he simply knew that God existed, and cared for him, David. After a lifetime of addressing the issue professionally, he concludes ' I can see no way whatever of proving the existence of God to everyone of reasonable intelligence and good will.' He therefore falls back on his original faith. He just knows. This is no doubt comforting for him, but not a lot of help to anyone else. Individual conviction is not a sound basis for proceeding. His argument seems to be that a God who was subject to human proof or disproof would not be God at all. Thus of course we cannot prove the negative case.

But if we do not accept this, we can point to grounds for disbelief (set out, for example very clearly by Richard Carrier at the website www.infidels.org). Propositions are offered about (the Christian) God that are not sustainable. For example, that God is omnipresent and has given us all the ability to know him. But while David Jenkins does, many do not – for my part I have no sense whatever of his existence. Again, there is the familiar point that God is all powerful, all knowing, and all compassionate, yet allows suffering to continue on a vast scale. And he is supposed to have made the universe for a moral purpose, whereas nature is clearly amoral, red in tooth and claw. The only answers to these arguments are entirely *ad hoc*, for example that God is really compassionate, but allows suffering for some inscrutable reason. Alister McGrath, professor of historical theology at Oxford, offers the argument that whenever there is human suffering, God suffers too. So that's all right then. Such arguments, even if they were sensible, are incapable of proof or disproof, and seem invented only to preserve the original idea. Since there is no positive proof, and several grounds for implausibility, it is reasonable not to believe in God.

Similarly one may say that while absence of evidence is not *proof* of absence (of whatever is being asserted) it is certainly evidence. Especially if the search for evidence is thorough and reliable. For example there is, as far as I know, no evidence that the Israelites travelled to America in ancient times, as Mormon doctrine holds, or that the Irish built the pyramids. The histories of both America and pyramids have been extensively researched. This does not absolutely prove these things did not happen. But it is a good basis for assuming they did not, at least until some positive evidence comes to light.

One should however point out that there are enquiries in which absence is sometimes confused with disproof. Thus the effects of treatments, or of harmful conditions, on health are commonly assessed statistically, using a sizable population. But a result that is significant statistically can arise either from there being a very small effect in many individuals, or from a range of effects, with most people being affected not at all or only slightly, and some few to an extent that is clinically important. In such cases, (apparent) absence of evidence may conceal a real presence. Psychologists stress, or should do, the importance of looking at individual differences.

56

TWENTY THINGS THEY NEVER SAID

If imitation is the sincerest form of flattery, misquotation must come pretty close. At least two factors are clearly at work. One is confabulation. This is the tendency to fill out, or even make up, something that makes sense, or sounds good, when the original cannot be recalled accurately. The other might be termed accretion, a tendency to attribute some saying, or indeed action, to a well-known figure rather than the real, less familiar, author of it.

The reputed origin of the quote may of course be either real or fictional. The latter is the easiest to check, since a fictional individual can only have said what his or her own author wrote. It is easy to find out what Tarzan actually said to Jane when they first met on screen, at least if one has access to the original film (*Tarzan, the Ape-Man*) of 1932. On the other hand, with real people there is always the possibility that the quote is something they actually did say at some time. No one has as yet had their entire life's utterances recorded, a notion for science fiction (for example the Matrix in *Dr Who*). Sometimes one can show that it was said, or written, but by someone else earlier. But often the best we can do is to say there is no evidence for it, perhaps supplemented by what would be termed 'internal evidence', that is the impression that it doesn't sound right for the alleged speaker. Or, in some cases, that the latter actually denied having said it. But of course they might be untruthful or forgetful.

Books have been compiled of distorted or false quotations, but here are just a few.

1. 'Me Tarzan, you Jane' is the supposed greeting of the ape-man to his future mate. In fact the exchange goes like this.
Jane: Jane.
Tarzan: Jane.
Jane: And you? You?
Tarzan: Tarzan! Tarzan!
Jane: Tarzan.
Tarzan: Jane. Tarzan. Jane. Tarzan.

2. 'Beam me up, Scotty' is the memorable command of Captain Kirk in the original televised *Star Trek* series. The nearest he ever came to it is actually 'Beam us up, Mr Scott'.

3. W.C. Fields is unforgettable, and his least forgettable of many lines is probably 'Any man who hates dogs and children can't be all bad'. Unfortunately it was said, not by him, but about him.

4. In contrast probably the only line remembered for Queen Marie Antoinette is 'Let them eat cake!', supposedly in response to reports that the peasants were clamouring for bread. There is no evidence that she did say it, it is almost certainly out of character, and it is recorded of at least one other person many years before.

5. Shakespeare's Hamlet is supposed to have said, 'Alas, poor Yorick! I knew him well', when contemplating a newly unearthed skull. Nearly. He says, 'Alas, poor Yorick! I knew him, Horatio – a fellow of infinite jest, of most excellent fancy.'

6. 'I have nothing to declare except my genius' is the well-known boast of Oscar Wilde when passing through Customs on landing in

America. This one is certainly in character, but there is no reliable evidence for it, and in only appeared in print many years later.

7. 'Nice guys finish last' is an appealingly cynical remark attributed to Leo Durocher, manager of the New York Giants baseball team What he appears to have said, in 1946, is 'The nice guys are all over there. In seventh place'.

8. Christian apologists are wont to claim that George Washington said, 'It is impossible to rightly govern the world without God and the Bible'. But there is no evidence that he did so.

9. 'Crisis? What crisis?' is supposed to have been said by Prime Minister James Callaghan in January 1979, in response to a charge that the country was facing 'mounting chaos'. Actually this was a headline in *The Sun*. What Callaghan said, admittedly less snappily, was apparently: 'I promise you that if you look at it from outside, and perhaps you're taking a rather parochial view at the moment, I don't think that other people in the world would share the view that there is mounting chaos.'

10. The Duke of Wellington was reported, by an officer who claimed to have overheard it, to have exclaimed, at a critical moment in the Battle of Waterloo, 'Up, Guards, and at them!' – or 'at 'em'. He later denied it.

11. 'Come with me to the Casbah!' is supposed to have been said by Charles Boyer to Hedy Lamarr (both no doubt now forgotten) in the film *Algiers* of 1938. He didn't, but the line was later included in at least one Loony Tunes cartoon.

12. 'I detest what you say, but I would fight to the death for your right to say it' is a rather noble if exaggerated sentiment often attributed to Voltaire. It's unlike the ultra-realistic Voltaire, and it can't be found in his writings.

13. Dr Samuel Johnson is the real author of many memorable quotes, but two it seems he did not produce are: 'Your manuscript

is both good and original. But the part that is good is not original, and the part that is original is not good'. And:

14. 'It is better to remain silent and be thought a fool, than to open your mouth and remove all doubt'. This is also attributed, equally uncertainly, to several other people, including Abraham Lincoln, Mark Twain and (of course) Oscar Wilde. Johnson did write, in one of his essays: 'It is observed somewhere, that few have repented of having forborne to speak'.

15. Galileo is supposed to have said, on his death-bed, '*epur si muove*' ('but it does move'), about his notion that the earth went round the sun, which he had been forced to recant by the religious authorities, under threat of torture. But it seems to be apocryphal.

16. Hundreds, probably, of more or less serious mimics have done James Cagney growling 'Ya dirty rat!'. Unfortunately he never did say it on film. The nearest was 'Mmm, that dirty, double-crossin' rat!', in *Blonde Crazy*, 1931.

17. Humphrey Bogart, in *Casablanca* (1942) never said 'Play it again, Sam.' He did say 'You played it for her, you can play it for me … If she can stand it, I can. Play it!. Also, 'Play it once Sam. For old times' sake...Play *As Time Goes By*.' Strange how many memorable but wrong quotes come from old films.

18. The words of Sherlock Holmes are enshrined in what aficionados know as the Sacred Canon, the four novels and fifty-six short stories about him by Sir Arthur Conan Doyle. Nowhere does Holmes make his most famous remark, 'Elementary, my dear Watson!' It sounds perfect, but the nearest thing is probably when Watson cries 'Excellent!', and Holmes replies simply, 'Elementary!' (in *The Crooked Man*).

19. 'There's a sucker born every minute' is attributed to Phineas T. Barnum, the American showman. Actually it was said by one David Hannum. A man called George Hull had created a fake fossilised giant, which proved a commercial success when put on

view. Hannum bought a share in the business, believing the giant to be genuine. By way of riposte, Barnum had another giant created, and denounced the original as a fake. Hannum's remark related to the punters who paid to see the Barnum giant, since he knew that he, Hannum, had the genuine article.

20. Abraham Lincoln has gathered to himself numerous profound sayings. Most people would probably be happy to agree that he said: 'You can fool some of the people all of the time, or all of the people some of the time, but you cannot fool all of the people all of the time'. Allegedly, it was in a speech in September 1858 in Clinton, Ohio. But it does not appear in the text printed in the local paper at the time. The best evidence for it seems to be that in 1910 two people recalled Lincoln saying it in 1856. Well, maybe, maybe not. Today's governments have discovered that it is not necessary anyway. You merely have to fool enough voters to swing marginal constituencies.

Those who care to pursue this game might like to seek out *They Never Said It*, by Paul F Boller and John George, 1990, or *Nice Guys Finish Seventh*, by Ralph Keyes, 1993.

John Radford, Emeritus Professor of Psychology at the University of East London, has led a quiet life as (mostly) an academic. He built up perhaps the largest Department of Psychology in the UK, and introduced Psychology into the GCE A-level. It is now one of the most popular subjects. He has researched and written on many subjects, including child prodigies, higher education, sex and gender differences, the psychology of religion, intelligence and personality, and Sherlock Holmes. He is a Fellow and Honorary Life Member of the British Psychological Society, a Chartered Psychologist, and a Fellow of the Royal Anthropological Institute. He is skeptical by nature, keen on discovering the facts rather than relying on myths, authorities and popular prejudices.

Donald Rooum had five minutes of fame in 1963, when he was arrested, charged with carrying a bit of brick to be used as an offensive weapon at a demonstration, and acquitted because the arresting officer, a Detective Sergeant, made a stupid mistake in planting the evidence. The case discredited the long-held magistrates' rule-of-thumb, that police evidence may be taken as true. At the time Donald was doing political cartoons for *Peace News* and *The Spectator*. These days he does a couple of regular strip cartoons, 'Wildcat' in *Freedom* since 1980, and 'Sprite' in *The Skeptic* since 1987. An amateur naturalist, he was awarded a first-class degree in Life Sciences by the Open University at the age of 51, and elected a Chartered Biologist and Member of the Institute of Biology at the age of 76.